FIRE IN THEIR BONES

THE TRUE STORY OF A MISSIONARY COUPLE'S FORTY YEARS IN AFRICA

BY PHILIP RANDALL
WITH GORDON AND GENEVA CHRISTENSEN

WIPF & STOCK · Eugene, Oregon

Wipf and Stock Publishers
199 W 8th Ave, Suite 3
Eugene, OR 97401

Fire in Their Bones
The True Story of a Missionary Couple's Forty Years in Africa
By Randall, Philip and Christensen, Gordon
Copyright©2001 by Randall, Philip

ISBN 13: 978-1-60608-185-3

Publication date 9/11/2008

Table of Contents

Introduction 5
Wrestling Not Against Flesh and Blood
    A vignette 7
Chapter 1
    Gordon's Rescue 11
Chapter 2
    Geneva's Childhood 25
Love and Trust
    A vignette 37
Chapter 3
    A Romance at North Park 41
Chapter 4
    Off to Africa 59
Facing Unknowns
    A vignette 67
Chapter 5
    Seeing God's Power 71
Chapter 6
    A Rough Start 77
Letters Home 91
Chapter 7
    A Revival in the Land 93
Chapter 8
    Evelyn's Legacy 113

CHAPTER 9
 INTO THE CLASSROOM 121
A GIFT OF RAIN
 A VIGNETTE 149
CHAPTER 10
 DISCIPLING DISCIPLERS 151
CHAPTER 11
 A NATION IN TURMOIL 159
CHAPTER 12
 DEEPER INTO CHAOS 175
CHAPTER 13
 GOOD COUNTRY AIR 195
CHAPTER 14
 MUSIC TO GOD'S EARS 203
CHAPTER 15
 SPIRITUALLY FILLED TO OVERFLOWING 217
CHAPTER 16
 A NEW WAR IN AFRICA 229
CHAPTER 17
 THE MOST VALUABLE HARVEST 249
CHAPTER 18
 COMMITTING TRUTHS TO PAPER 255
CHAPTER 19
 WATCHING THE SPIRIT MOVE 261
CHAPTER 20
 JUST SAYING NO TO ROCKING CHAIRS 269

Introduction

Biographers love to write about the rich and famous. Readers are already familiar with the subject and have an interest in the life story. The marketing's done! So the biographer gets out in front of the audience and supplies the demand.

This formula sells. It's why the biographies are about Churchill and Ike, not Kilroy.

Yet the formula misses so much. There are many more people out there living remarkable lives than the tiny percentage who are rich and famous. What about the people who had the courage to *fight* the deciding war, or the skill to *build* the seven wonders of the world?

Now take the question a step further, and you get to the *really big* unknowns: What about the people who build the Kingdom of God — the ones who've gotten hold of the blueprint and are laying the bricks? These are the lives that are quietly changing the world, and eternity. Who are they?

I have long been intrigued about the lives that, unrecognized by the world, moved the Kingdom of God forward through the ages. There are the 40 or 50 who, working independently over thousands of years, produced a seamless communication called the Bible. There are the anonymous monks, who, through the Dark Ages, kept it from being lost. There are the unknown Anabaptists, jailed, hurt and ridiculed in colonial America, who insisted that freedom of religion be a part of the new nation so the message could be preached unfettered. There are the revivalists of the 1800s who spread the message across the land.

These are lives that usually pass silently through this world, unnoticed. They help shape eternity while the world dwells on the rich and famous.

These are the really big stories, and I wondered if I would have to get to heaven to hear about God's agents on Earth, the ones who actually got on the track and ran the race Paul urged be run.

I think Gordon and Geneva Christensen live this kind of life. They are not rich or famous, but they did get ahold of the blueprint and get acquainted with mortar.

Our paths crossed in the early 1990s in St. Petersburg, Florida. I quickly realized there was a lot to learn from Gordon and Geneva. If you never meet them in person, let me describe what I observed:

The vibrancy of their lives stands out. Their eyes shine with joy. They are modest and approachable and friendly, and there is something notable about them. You sense it. They have a Godly imprint on their souls that is discernible.

I think these are two of the kinds of lives I had wondered about for years. And I think God, knowing the desire of my heart, honored it by bumping me into Gordon and Geneva Christensen. He didn't make me wait to encounter a few of His agents on Earth, ones who quietly made the plan happen while everyone else was at the movies.

Because I believe God did me this favor, I have attempted to offer, in the following chapters, vignettes and life lessons, a glimpse at the lives of two people who answered the call, who ran the race, who joyfully helped lay the bricks of the Kingdom.

Philip Randall
November 1999

Wrestling Not Against Flesh And Blood

A Vignette

The small prop plane bounced to a stop on the dusty jungle runway and delivered the last group of passengers being ferried to this remote village in the Congo.

This was the deep jungle, unmapped even now in the 1970s, the territory of a tribe called the Pakabetis who until two years earlier had been unreached by the Christian missionaries. These Africans had been sent decades earlier into this forgotten part of jungle, cast out by the long-gone colonial Belgian government that had found them too difficult to deal with.

Missionary and teacher Gordon Christensen was the leader of this arriving group of five African seminary students. He had planned a week of field training for these young men who desired to become village pastors. Gordon was accompanied by his wife, Geneva, not only a trained nurse who could meet most of the medical needs of the villagers, but also a person especially adept at reaching African women with the Gospel.

These two were seasoned veterans of African missionary work. Gordon, at 42, was a lean, black-haired man with a smile quick to flash and an enthusiasm for the Gospel that hardship hadn't extinguished. Geneva, a mother of three, was a slender woman whose calm demeanor belied a genuine toughness forged in Dust Bowl Kansas and sharpened by a lifelong commitment to be a missionary.

They were a pair who had felt the call to Christian service since their childhoods, .and they had answered. Along the way there had been poverty, polio, plane crashes, evacuations, guns in the face, family lives in the balance, and lives taken. There had been exhaustion and discouragement.

There also had been a lot of help, all through their lives, from others who stopped to care for them at the perfect moment. There had been inspiring examples of courage and love that strengthened them. There had been joys and victories so sweet, Godly reassurances so life-changing, manifestations of God's power so moving, that there was no price too high to pay to be where they were at this time. They had lived through a lot of adventures.

But this trip wasn't expected to be one of them. It looked like a routine mission trip in which Gordon, Geneva and their students would minister, learn, and grow a little more.

They were wrong. What they were really in for was a fight.

It was a fight that Gordon and Geneva had been in preparation for all their lives. They didn't know it at the time. And they didn't know it now, but these would be the deciding hours.

At stake was a forgotten village full of forgotten lives. But the skirmish over it would be intense. On one side was an evil so ugly and powerful that it terrorized even these strong hunters and crushed them under its oppression. On the other side was God, who says He so loves these forgotten people that He sent his only begotten Son to die for them — and now these ambassadors to claim them.

It was a D-Day unrealized. The decades of personal preparation and trials would be put to the harshest test in the hours ahead. But this wasn't a George Patton, who had trained all his life for the day he would face a Rommel in deciding battle for Africa or Europe. This was a missionary couple with no physical firepower but a lot of spiritual power.

And the fight wasn't for all of Europe, or Africa. Heaven and hell were about to throw all they had into a war for a village. The weapons would be different, but Gordon and Geneva understood them. The outcome wouldn't be headline news, but two spiritual domains were poised and watching intensely.

The small plane's prop spun to life with a roar, and the pilot turned it back onto the runway, sped down it and disappeared over the trees.

Gordon, Geneva, and the five students were greeted by some villagers and a very worried village pastor, a former elephant hunter named Boko, who told Gordon there were big problems in the village.

The group walked toward the huts and into the fray.

* * * *

This book is about the life journey of two missionaries, Gordon and Geneva Christensen, as well as the people who inspired them, the values that guided them, the events that shaped them and the God who guided them to a very high calling.

It's also about *how*. How they did what they did and fulfilled the New Testament promise that we can be more than conquerors through Christ who loves us.

Gordon sits between his Grandma Weston and mother, Helen, about 1930 at Alki Beach, Washington. Standing is his brother, Ernest.

Chapter 1

Gordon's Rescue

For 7-year-old Gordon Christensen and his brother, Ernest, a big day in Depression-era Seattle meant going to a hillside overlooking the giant Boeing plant and waiting to see a plane take off. The brothers would pack a lunch, go through the woods to their grassy observation point and wait for the free show. A biplane would taxi down the runway and take off with a roar for a test flight, or a twin-engine plane would be rolled out of a hangar and into the sun. It was thrilling to a kid; the sights and sounds fueled Gordon's imagination. What would it be like to fly? To go on adventures in a machine like that, to go anywhere he wanted?

But within a couple hours, the imaginary flights were over, and it was back to earth and the harsh realities of home life.

Life was very harsh for the Christensens in those days. The boys' father, Ivor, had moved with his wife from British Columbia in the early 1920s. He had joined the U.S. Army during World War I in hopes that service in Europe would win him citizenship in the U.S. It worked. Ivor and his wife, Helen Violet, moved to 7502 Renton Avenue, the "wrong side of the tracks" in Seattle. There Ivor could find the carpentry jobs that had dried up in British Columbia. In booming Seattle during the 1920s, it was easy to find the day-by-day construction work that kept the family going.

But it wasn't easy being an immigrant there, and Ivor had a heavy Swedish accent that marked him. Swedes, newcomers to the Northwest, were looked down upon in south Seattle. They were "dumb Swedes" with accents that caused words like "Jell-O" to come out, "Yello."

The ostracism hurt Ivor deeply. He was ashamed of his Swedish heritage. He told people he was Canadian, which was true, but it left out the fact that he was born in Sweden — in Luleo in the province of Norland — and came to Canada as a boy. Even his children didn't know the whole truth until they were much older. But the denial did not help Ivor shake his sense of rejection in Seattle. He had been ostracized all his life.

In 1925, while the family was still getting established in its new country, Gordon was born. He was the third child. His sister, Kathleen, and brother, Ernest, had been born in British Columbia.

Ivor's father, whose last name was Bergstrom, was the owner of a logging company in Sweden. When the company went bankrupt in the late 1800s, Bergstrom hoped to get a new start in the "new land." He came to the United States alone, leaving his wife and children until he could send for them.

The new land was not a land of milk and honey for many immigrants, but very hard. Bergstrom finally was able to send for his family, but by that time, he had become an alcoholic, and before his family ever laid eyes on him in the new land, he disappeared.

Mrs. Bergstrom and her children arrived in New York City as an abandoned family. She never saw her husband again. And in a strange country with no support, it wasn't long until she had to have others care for her children. The older children, including Ivor, went to live with an aunt in British Columbia. Ivor's older sister, Viola, cast in a sort of mother's role for the boys, realized quickly that even with an aunt's help, she couldn't raise the two boys who had come with her. In British Columbia, Ivor, age 8, and his brother, Henry, were offered for adoption and taken in by a Danish schoolteacher named Christensen. Viola kept four little sisters with her and raised them.

So Ivor Christensen had known family breakup, abandonment and rejection — ostracism — all his life. Thus, when he was a father, raising a family in Seattle, he was a dark, brooding man. He was not a cruel man — he didn't physically harm his wife or children — but he was distant, harsh with his words, never affectionate.

This was the cold, hard stage on which Gordon started life.

Gordon can recall only once sitting in his father's lap, to get a lesson about telling time on a clock. Being that near his father was so unusual that it made him uneasy.

When the Great Depression hit in 1929, life for the Christensens got even harder. The daily hunt for work became much tougher for Ivor. He began drinking. Gordon would see his father come home after a day's work and head straight for the basement for a drink of whatever he had there. As time passed, the drinking got worse. Arguments in the house could be horrible. The emotional abuse could become frightening, and soon, when Ivor came home and headed for the basement, young Gordon and Ernest headed for the woods.

There were plenty of woods and open spaces for them. Renton Avenue was in its "young family" stage, and there were many children around. An open field nearby was ideal for football and baseball. The turmoil at home made it easy to stay outdoors, playing with the other kids.

But running with the kids was not a good idea, even in the early 1930s. Years later, Gordon would recall that by the time he was 8, his language was as "foul as a pit," courtesy of the example of his friends and his environment.

"I knew more at 8 years of age than most kids ought to know at 16. What I didn't know, the rest of the kids were trying to teach me."

Looking back on those years, Gordon is amazed that he ever escaped the failure that seemed planned for him from birth, and describes it as miraculous — a gift of God.

How did he beat the odds against him?

First, Gordon was born in the midst of a great Christian revival in the U.S.. Churches were emphasizing evangelism. Crusades from coast to coast were drawing thousands and changing their lives. So profound was the impact that among Swedish immigrants, it was not uncommon to greet each other on the street with, "How is your walk (with the Lord)?"

Second, the field where Gordon played also became the site from which the First Covenant Church of Seattle began youth outreach. There was an old building foundation on the lot. It sagged in the middle and would fill with water in the winter, becoming the children's ice skating rink. But the old foundation also became one of the touchstones for the church and the neighborhood children.

Third, Gordon received a new role model: his Sunday school teacher, Evert Bjordahl. Evert not only taught lessons from the Bible, but he and his class had some sort of outing each week. They might go together for a ferry ride on Puget

Sound. The first restaurant meal Gordon ever ate, complete with big napkins and menus, was when he was about 10 years old, courtesy of Evert, who took the class for supper once when he had been doing well in his business as a piano teacher.

The First Covenant Church of Seattle was an elaborate downtown church, but it reached to the outskirts of Seattle, such as Renton Avenue. First Covenant launched a Sunday school program in the neighborhood. Church members rented a dance hall in Hillman City, a little trading post near Gordon's home, and would clean it for their use each week. A friend of Gordon's named Don Covey was the first to start attending. Since he was the star fullback of the sandlot football team, Don's absence scuttled any games on Sunday mornings, so Gordon and Ernest started going along with him.

Gordon was immediately drawn to the love and laughter he found in the Sunday school program. It was a needed contrast to home.

"It was exciting," Gordon says. "They didn't have any kind of sermon. Just Sunday school. More and more children came until they had 50 to 60 people there."

Evert ended each class with an invitation to receive Christ, saying he always had time to talk with kids about it afterward. After about three or four months of attendance, Gordon asked Evert to pray with him, and he did.

"That was the beginning," Gordon says. "I suppose a lot of things had been building up to that day. One of them was that I sensed a spirit in that place that I had never sensed before, and that was love. I sensed that these people really did love one another, and in my family, we didn't know the meaning of the word. We were 'sociable'; we weren't always tooth and claw with one another, but we really didn't know the meaning of what they were exemplifying, which was true Christian love. To have people smiling, happy, glad to be doing what they were doing. Appreciative of us kids, loving us. It was amazing. And so, I think that was the main thing that led me to ask him that day."

After that prayer with Evert, Gordon was elated. He went home for dinner, and his happiness must have shown. Everyone at the table stared at him. Finally, somebody — he doesn't remember who — asked him, "Did you get saved?" Gordon said yes.

His whole family looked at him. "Why did you do a dumb thing like that?" he was asked.

That was his introduction to life as a Christian, and it exemplified what family life was going to be like for him from then on. At age 10, Gordon was out of step with his family and was going to stay that way for the rest of his youth. Even his father was critical of his faith; Ivor was vocally opposed to anything "religious."

Nevertheless, Sunday school became Gordon's mainstay. He continued attending each week and going with Evert and his class on outings or to visit the big church downtown for special music services. Evert was providing Gordon with a new circle of friends, Christian fellowship and Bible knowledge.

But about six months after he started attending the Sunday school, Gordon feared he might have to leave it. Ivor received a job offer to work on Grand Coulee Dam, which was about 265 miles away. Gordon was told the whole family was moving.

It was a moment of crisis for young Gordon. He was going to be pulled away from Sunday school and his new friends. Gordon walked out to the woods behind his house, got down on his knees and asked God to change his father's mind.

Shortly thereafter, Gordon's words came ringing back to him in a way that taught him forever that God answers prayer.

"I still remember that day," Gordon says. "As I walked back up to our front porch, Dad came out and said, 'Your mother and I have changed our minds. You can stay with your grandma and grandpa for the school year.' That was my first big answer to prayer."

Gordon moved in with his Grandma and Grandpa Weston in Seattle. That extra year with his grandparents and his new circle of friends was very important to establishing his faith.

In that year Gordon became eligible for confirmation at the church. He was voted to be the speaker at the service, a great honor that excited him. He wanted a nice set of clothes to wear for the service, and wrote to his father asking for the money. The nicest thing he had to wear was a black zipper jacket. But his father said no. Gordon was crushed. He spent the night crying in bed and thinks his grandmother wept too, outside his door. But Gordon went to the confirmation and gave his speech, wearing his black zipper jacket.

After confirmation and later that summer, Gordon packed up and joined his family at Grand Coulee Dam. It was a trial for him. Many of the people at the First Covenant Church of Seattle told Gordon they would be praying for him while he was gone, and he thinks that is what helped him through the rough time ahead.

At Grand Coulee, Gordon could not find the kind of church he had come from. The only fellowship he could find seemed preoccupied with internal problems and dwindling numbers.

He had no support at home. He had to sleep in a bed with his brother, who would complain bitterly when Gordon tried to have a private devotion at night by reading the Bible in bed with a flashlight.

He found no Christian friend that he can remember.

Gordon recalls his time at Grand Coulee as a two-year no-growth period. The only good thing about it is when it ended and the family returned to Seattle, he still had his faith.

First Covenant Church continued to fill a big void in his life. When Gordon was about 11, he began attending summer camps at Covenant Beach Bible Camp in Des Moines, Washington. These camps built many enjoyable memories for Gordon, including being baptized in Puget Sound about age 14. But meeting and talking to visiting missionaries made the biggest impression on him.

Gordon remembers meeting Ralph Hanson, who later became world missions secretary for the Evangelical Covenant Church of America. He had fascinating stories of trying to reach the people of Alaska with the Gospel. To reach the wilds of the Alska territory, he had built an airplane with skis. It was a cutting edge ministry, and it fired Gordon's imagination.

Gordon also remembered Emory Lindgren, who had served in Alaska. He was a young, personable, adventure-loving man with plenty of good stories to tell.

"One thing I will always thank God for is the church always sent lively, young, personable missionaries who made you feel like it wouldn't be impossible for you to be a missionary," Gordon says.

Bible camp was a big factor in his deciding to become a missionary. But the example of his own family also was key. Gordon could look at the men in his family, see what they were becoming, and see what he would probably become. Why not live fully committed to God? Why not dedicate his life to serving Him? The life he saw around him would lead nowhere, to nothing.

His grandfather Weston also had become an alcoholic. He had been saved while serving in the British Army during World War I through the ministry of the Salvation Army. He apparently maintained his walk until the Depression years, when there was very little work. He and Ivor would make home brew. It was their escape from daily life, but it was also Weston's undoing. Gordon remembers in his teen years finding Grandpa Weston passed out on a pathway leading to his house. Gordon gathered him up and got him home. Weston worked as a gardener in Seattle, and at this point in his life would often spend his wages on liquor.

Alcohol and discord dominated the family. Gordon remembers Christmas and New Year's keg parties at his house, with dancing into the early morning hours. It upset Gordon, and he would go to bed, much to others' bewilderment.

This was the life Gordon saw as opposed to the lives he saw through church and Bible camp. It was a stark contrast to the influential men, including the owner of a key lumber company in Seattle, who would stand in church and give their testimonies, sometimes even expressing their love for the Lord with tears in their eyes.

As Gordon neared college age, his father made him an offer. If he would study architecture — become the one reading the plans instead of hammering the nails — Ivor would pay the bill. But for any other line of study, he would not help.

Gordon decided that he wanted to be a missionary. As he neared graduation, he set his sites on Seattle Pacific University in Seattle to begin his college education and North Park College, the Covenant Church's college in Chicago, to finish it.

But again, as it had been since he was 10, Gordon had to face his father's disapproval: Missionary work or the clergy was a sure road to poverty. Gordon was being foolish. Establish a respectable profession. Be somebody. And Ivor meant what he said; there would be no help from him if Gordon pursued his own goal.

What huge pressure for a 17-year-old to face! Yet it would pale in comparison to what lay ahead.

Gordon turned 18 the summer before he started at Seattle Pacific University. He got a job loading and unloading lumber at a construction site where his father was working. At summer's end, he quit to go to college the next day. It had been exhausting work, and the next morning as he headed for the campus, he was surprised at how tired he was. He had to climb part of a hill between Second and Fourth avenues in Seattle to catch a bus and was worn out by the time he got to the bus stop.

At Seattle Pacific, he could barely stand in line to enroll in classes. At home that night, his fatigue got even worse. He felt like there were needles stabbing him in the neck. By the next morning, he was stiff and feeling numb. There were slight signs of paralysis. The family called a doctor to come to the house.

After the examination, Gordon's mother came into his room in tears. "You have polio" she told him.

Gordon didn't take it very seriously. "It's just another thing I'll get over," he thought.

Polio was sweeping the Puget Sound area. There were more than 1,000 cases that summer, and Gordon was taken with many of the other patients to Harbor View Hospital for medical care. Gordon's left arm was paralyzed. Yet he felt fortunate as he lay in that hospital ward for six weeks. Others were in iron lungs, so paralyzed that they could not breathe without aid. He heard the repetitive hiss of compressed air day and night as others struggled for every breath.

Gordon was later transferred to Swedish Hospital, where he saw the full extent of the paralysis on his left side.

It was a time of serious prayer for Gordon. His youthful bravado about polio had evaporated as he realized how destructive the disease was. "God, you've got to heal me if I'm going to be a missionary," he prayed.

This was the time of most serious struggle for Gordon. He saw patient after patient brought into the ward, some almost unable to move at all. But he did not harbor worries about how the disease would affect his personal plans. "I was just leaving it up to the Lord," he says. "If he wanted me to be a missionary, he had to put some strength into that leg, particularly."

The public was very afraid of polio. Because doctors weren't sure how it was transmitted, people stayed away from the hospital. Gordon's former Sunday school teacher, Evert, was an exception.

Evert visited Gordon regularly at the hospital and prayed for him. Evert also got other people praying for Gordon. He contacted every prayer chain he could think of. So even while Gordon's family did not believe in prayer, there was much prayer for him. Evert contacted other churches and ministries and urged them to pray for Gordon, including the Assembly of God Church and a ministry on First Avenue in Seattle called Brother Jack's.

Gordon was overjoyed to see slight signs of recovery. About 12 weeks after he was first admitted to the hospital, he was able to walk out. At home, his mother continued the hot pack treatments that forced his muscles to relax and contract as they warmed and cooled. His mother put the very hot towels on him every two hours all day for the next six weeks, while he slowly tried to work his way through his paralysis.

Gordon did so by trying to play the piano in the living room, thinking "thumb," or "forefinger," and seeing them twitch slightly. Gordon, who describes himself as a persistent "plodder," sat at the piano for hours. Eventually, he could move his wrist. Then he could push down a key with his finger. While he was resting, Gordon found inspiration in the book *Ben Hur*. The story of a Roman citizen who finds wholeness in Christ, despite a hostile society and embittering personal tragedies, touched him deeply during the long hours of each day. The story and its message helped re-energize him for another bout with the piano. In time, like Ben Hur, Gordon found freedom.

Several weeks after getting out of the hospital, Gordon was able to return to his church for a young people's meeting.

He was greeted warmly, and many were surprised to see him there, though most everyone had been following his recovery. Gordon says it was the prayers his Sunday school teacher urged that released the power of God for his restoration, "and the answers to prayer were progressive. Little by little."

Gordon re-enrolled at Seattle Pacific College the following spring. During that term he was praying much about his future and what he should be doing, and he felt a definite leading to enroll in North Park College & Seminary, the Covenant Church's seminary in Chicago. Gordon announced his plans. His church friends were very supportive, but his father was as adamant as ever that Gordon was making a big mistake.

LIFE LESSONS

One of the things Gordon Christensen says he took away from his childhood is the lesson that Jesus Christ is the only true security in life, and faith in Jesus Christ and a commitment to walk with him is the only road to success.

Gordon stood in stark contrast to his father, who also had a very difficult childhood. Ivor Christensen was in essence an abandoned child, and he struggled with the consequence of bitterness and insecurity the rest of his life. When he met his hardships without Jesus, the wounds he suffered never healed. As a result, his emotional detachment and harshness threatened to leave his children abandoned as well, even though he was physically present. His alcohol abuse, verbal abuse and heavy-handedness threatened to trap his own children in a similar life.

It was as a boy that Ivor discovered his father was gone, and as a boy that Gordon discovered he had a heavenly Father. A trail of family ruin — laid two generations earlier when Grandpa Bergstrom turned to alcohol and then decided to leave his family — was detoured by a child's realization that Jesus Christ is the Savior.

Grandpa Weston also had made this discovery and had walked with the Lord for years. But certain pressures he faced, perhaps the pressure of emigrating to Canada from England, or trying to earn a living through the Depression, caused him to lose sight of what Gordon was seeing — Jesus Christ is the key to salvation and success. One problem might have been in his earlier years of marriage, his wife was not supportive of his calls for family church attendance. There was not a like-mindedness between husband and wife that perhaps was the root cause of his later problems, but that is speculation, and it could be unfair to Grandma Weston.

By the time Gordon came to live with them while his family was at Grand Coulee Dam, Grandma Weston was more supportive of his spiritual growth than Grandpa Weston was. She was the one who was supportive of his confirmation — Grandpa Weston didn't care, as Gordon remembers. She was the one Gordon remembers as full of laughter and merriment — traits he treasured and needed to see as a boy even though she was married to an alcoholic who rejected the church and lost his witness for Jesus Christ.

Thus, another lesson Gordon learned from his childhood is that there is a devil with a threefold ministry: to steal, kill and destroy. This evil enemy is not above attacking children in their most formative years so the negative consequences can reverberate for generations. He attacks parents and inspires bad decisions that can harm their children, grandchildren, great-grandchildren and beyond. He will try to drag down Christians who have walked with the Lord but faint under the trials of life.

Those trials are a fact of life, and the attacks are common to mankind. They surface in ways such as a child's announcement at the dinner table that he has been saved, only to be slapped with, "Why did you do a dumb thing like that?" They surface with a family's decision to move to a spiritual desert before that child's roots in the faith are secure. The attack can be through the daily example from authority figures on how to live wrongly. It can come in the form of enticement (a free ticket to college if you won't go into Christian ministry) or pressure (a polio attack once a decision had been made to go on the mission field).

But Jesus is the key to salvation and success.

When he looks back, Gordon sees that God made a way where there was no way. There was a church that cared about evangelism and made efforts to reach children. There was a Sunday school teacher who went above and beyond the call of duty. There were summer church camps where inspiring missionaries effectively communicated their enthusiasm for the mission. There were services where pillars of the Seattle society would speak unashamedly for the Lord. There was light at the end of the tunnel. The light was Jesus Christ.

Geneva's childhood home, the Noren farm near Oberlin Kansas.

Chapter 2

Geneva's Childhood

A childhood spent on a 240-acre Kansas farm in the 1930s is just one of the blessings God has given Geneva Christensen in her life.

It wasn't the easiest way to grow up; 240 acres wasn't much of a farm even in good years, but during the Dust Bowl of the '30s, crops were nonexistent. One year, Geneva's family had to survive on an annual income of $100. Yet as she looks back on those years, she sees them as God-ordained. It was His training ground for a family whose members would learn for a lifetime that He was ever-present, ever-loving and always the supplier of their needs. It was a time of shaping character that would be vital for what lay ahead, and of teaching the importance of family.

Geneva was born at the family farmhouse on Oct. 6, 1925, the third of David and Amanda Noren's four children. It was a time when no one in that area near Oberlin, Kansas, seemed to have much money, but the Norens were among the poorest of all. David Noren had been raised on an Iowa farm, the son of a Covenant pastor. It had been part of his family obligation to help keep that farm, but it meant that as a young man, he had earned almost no money to put toward a farm of his own. While working in the harvest fields in Kansas, he met the Carlson family and Amanda. Several years later, he asked for her hand in marriage, and in 1921, at the ages of 31 and 21, David and Amanda started a farm and family of their own.

The little farm they bought was down in a valley, near a creek and hills, not far from Amanda's parents. David knew from the beginning that this wasn't going to be the easiest place to farm, but he told Amanda that it was the people in the area, their friendliness and concern for one another, that made him want to live in Kansas.

In 1922 their first child, Evelyn, was born, followed by Edwin in 1923 or '24, Geneva in 1925 and Willard in 1927.

This was a very committed Christian family, although the church folk might have thought otherwise. Because it cost too much to drive the car, the family couldn't afford to go to town and to church in the same week. So one week they went to town, or David would go alone, and the other week they went to church. It was always a joy when church week rolled around, but the off-Sundays also were observed as a day of worship and rest. After morning chores were done, the Norens would put on good clothes and Mrs. Noren would put a nice tablecloth on the table, and the family would have a morning worship service, including music. David Noren never had music lessons, but he learned to play the violin, mandolin and autoharp. For a while, a neighbor loaned them a pump organ, which Mrs. Noren would play. They would sing, have a scripture reading, prayer, more singing, and then Mrs. Noren would go to the kitchen, stoke up the wood stove and get dinner started.

The Noren children in 1928. From left are Geneva, Edwin, baby Willard and Evelyn.

The family also broke some other traditions that probably elicited frowns: They played on Sunday afternoon instead of simply sitting, which was the custom. Geneva said her father, who had done his share of sitting as a preacher's son, said that sitting around gave him headaches. He had to be doing something. So Sunday afternoons were the time for family baseball, and the Noren pasture became the area hangout for kids who came over to join the game, or to pitch horseshoes. Mrs. Noren came out and played, too.

When the playing was done, she would always have something to drink as well as cookies or coffee bread. However, Mrs. Noren was a soul winner above all. Those Sunday baseball games, or winter domino or ping pong games played on the dining room table (which practically filled the room from wall to wall when it was stretched out for a game) became a contact point with those young people. Sooner or later she would have a talk with each one about the Lord. She would also talk to their parents.

Geneva remembers her mother going to visit the neighbors, or saying, "Today I feel I really need to confront (some acquaintance) about his soul." Her life was filled with the love of God. The Christian faith was woven so deeply into her and her family's life, it was a part of every day.

It was this kind of fun that overshadowed the family's poverty. The kids never thought of themselves as poor. They worked hard on the farm; everyone had chores. But Dave and Amanda always made sure there was respite from the work. For example, they would tell the children, "Today we're going to work hard, but this evening we're going to go fishing." Then after the day of work, they would head for the fishing hole. The parents made life on the farm enjoyable.

This was the home life that inspired three of the four Noren children to enter the mission field and one to serve the Lord at home. It had nothing to do with abundance; they had none. It had nothing to do with church attendance or keeping church traditions. Such devotion sprang from the genuineness of David and Amanda's faith, their prayers for their children before they were even born — offering them to God — and their faithfulness in day-to-day living.

It certainly didn't come through a life without stress. Geneva said it wasn't until she was much older that she learned that her father's nighttime walks in the the barn were hours of worry about finances. There was one time of trouble that, for Geneva, became a defining point of her life.

Dave had gotten a job as a county trustee, which brought in a little income for the family. One of his duties was to poison prairie dogs, which in the dry years would take over entire fields.

He was putting poison in a field and didn't notice the dust clouds rolling in from the south. The clouds of red dirt always churned out of Oklahoma, to the south, and would pick up momentum until the sun was darkened. These storms could be deadly. Children and old people were known to have died from inhaling so much dust that they developed "dust pneumonia," and cattle died of dirt-impacted stomachs from foraging for food through the dust.

When Dave looked up, he was already in the middle of a dust storm that he could not see through. He lost his bearings and had no idea where the car was. It was like being in a blizzard. He could see nothing at all through the darkness. He stopped and had no idea what he should do. He started praying for guidance.

Mrs. Noren was at home. Dave should have been back by then, and she had an idea what had happened. She gathered the four children around the trunk in the living room, and the family started praying for Dave.

Mrs. Noren also lit a kerosene lamp and put it in the window, even though he probably wouldn't be able to see it until he was about 5 feet from the glass.

Eventually they heard the sound of Dave's Ford coming toward the house, and they began rejoicing. Dad had gotten home.

He came in with quite a story to tell. He had been stuck in the middle of that field and was praying. In the midst of his prayer, as if by revelation, he had a sense to start walking in a certain direction. He started walking that way, although he could not tell which way it was. He kept going, and then the car appeared before him.

Geneva never forgot that episode. It impressed on her how powerful God is, and it greatly strengthened the faith of her whole family. The story became a reference point for all of them. It became the time God showed the Norens, from youngest to oldest, that He does answer prayer.

LIFE LESSONS

In addition to a family focused on God, Geneva found the hardships of the times to have been the best thing for her. It was like a boot camp for successful living. Among the lessons that came out of it:

SHARING — This family of six lived in a two-bedroom house. One of the bedrooms was no bigger than 8 feet by 12 feet. Everyone had to learn to live in close quarters and rub shoulders. Since there were two boys and two girls, the kids took turns on who would get a bedroom and who would sleep on a foldout davenport in the living-dining room. "We never had the privilege of having much privacy or our own rooms when we were growing up," she recalled in a 1994 interview. "Yet I have thought today that sometimes, I think some of our young people would do better in their marriages if early on in their lives they wouldn't have had their own private room and a private bathroom, because today young people do not learn how to cooperate . . . that was essential in our household. You just took turns, that's all. So it can be a good thing."

MODERATION — The food the family raised in a summer garden was what went on the table during the winter. There was one trip to town every other week, period. The family simply could not afford to be wasteful or indulgent with anything. David told Geneva when she had grown up that not being able to give more to his children was one of the hardest things for him to endure, because he naturally tended toward being an indulgent dad. To her, his words were reaffirmation that she was born in exactly the right time and right place to fulfill God's plan for her. Habits born of abundance would have been a stumbling block for her for the rest of her life. She would have to be tougher than that to get through her life, and she was prepared to be so from childhood.

Yet "moderation" and "self-denial" did not translate into "Spartan" or "harsh" regarding the family atmosphere.

Geneva's Childhood

Childhood was truly fun for Geneva. That is a credit to the love of her parents and their willingness to be avowedly God-dependent rather than self-sufficient. The family was focused on God, not problems. However, childhood was also filled with learning how to get home in a dust storm ("Find the wire fence across from the schoolhouse and follow it home," David told the kids. "It will bring you out near the stock tank near the house.") and coping with other intense hardships with a Christian code of conduct that included caring for others, valuing family relationships, and most importantly, valuing your relationship with God.

WORK — Working and earning money were a part of life even in childhood. Helping a neighbor around the house for a summer could earn enough to buy a new pair of shoes. And there was always work to be done on their own farm. The children practiced stewardship in their day-to-day living.

Every Christmas, Grandpa Noren would send each grandchild a dollar. One year, David told the children that if they wanted, he would put their money together and get them a ewe; they could start a sheep flock as a business. The kids said yes, and with the money David bought them a pregnant ewe that gave birth to twins. It was the beginning of quite a flock, which not only gave the boys work and taught everyone business skills, but also provided much of the money needed for the kids to go to high school (a big expense in those times — the kids had to move away from home and take an apartment in town to attend classes). In high school, Geneva would babysit until midnight for a quarter. That would buy lunch meat for a week. Everyone worked and earned.

PRAYER — It was part of each day. To have a prayerful family can be a blessing for generations to come.

Mrs. Noren's parents lived about 12 miles away, and Geneva often spent weekends or afternoons with them. They had devotions every morning. Grandpa read in Swedish, and Geneva used Swedish in their home.

When he prayed, Grandpa remembered everybody. The children always knew Grandpa and Grandma were praying for them.

"I remember Grandma saying, 'With the grandchildren and great-grandchildren, my prayer list is getting too long, that's all I have time to do in the morning,'" Geneva says. "It was interesting to find in her Bible after she passed away that she not only read the Bible but had study notes jotted down, and I hadn't realized Grandma was that kind of student of the Word."

CARE ABOUT PEOPLE MORE THAN GOODS — When David worked as a county trustee, he was responsible to deliver care boxes to needy families. He hated the program, because he thought it was abused. He refused to sign up for it himself. However, once he came home with several grocery boxes he was going to deliver to people better off than the Norens. "Kids, I want you to look in here," he told the children. Geneva remembers seeing a box of cold cereal — a luxury they could never afford — some oranges, apples and a candy bar. These were all big treats.

"If you would like to have a care box like this, I am willing to go and sign up. It is not right for me to withhold this from you, just because I see this program being misused. Because we honestly qualify."

This is how Geneva recalls their response: "'No Dad,' we said, 'We know this would hurt you a lot to have to go down there and sign up.' We would rather eat the homemade bread, which was more nutritious for us anyway, and our homemade cereal."

The children's first big step away from home was their entrance to Decatur County Community High School. The buses did not run out as far as the Noren farm, so the kids had to rent an apartment to live in during the week and go home on weekends.

There were many expenses for this "free" education. Besides the apartment, the family also had to pay for books.

To cover expenses, the children all held jobs in addition to attending classes. The two boys found plenty of work, while Geneva and Evelyn made money baby-sitting and participating in a paid teacher-assistance program in school. They bought and prepared their own meals and ran their own home as high school students.

But the big excitement of each weekend was not the Friday night football game or a social event. It was seeing Dad's old car pull up outside the basement apartment where they lived. "He'd always be there ready to take us home for the weekend," Geneva recalls. "That was the real joy for us. Once in awhile we would stay in for a game, but rarely, because it was more important for us to be together as a family."

Decisions about such things as spending weekends with family seem little in themselves, but they speak volumes about core values that can mean the difference between a victorious and defeated life. The Norens chose to support and be with each other rather than pursue self-interests, and they were rewarded with a family love and closeness that many families today struggle to achieve.

SEEKING GOD'S WILL — To see now the course Geneva took with her life, it's amusing that one of the decisions she wrestled with the most as a child was whether to commit her life to Christ. This little girl from Kansas was a tougher sell for Jesus than you would expect.

Even as a small child, Geneva sensed a call on her life to be a missionary. She struggled with this burden, which she recognized even before she was school age, because she was deeply concerned about being separated from her family. It kept her from surrendering her heart to the Lord at an early age, because she felt she couldn't ask Him to save her and not be willing to do what He asked of her. "Sometimes we don't give little kids much credit for comprehending these things, but I know that at a very early age I realized it would be unfair to say, 'Jesus, save me so I don't go to hell, but don't ask me to do something I don't want to do.' For that reason,

I did not surrender to the Lord until I was about 12 years old."

She kept her sense of calling to herself. She didn't even tell her parents what she expected to do with her life.

"I knew desperately that by being called to missions and not sharing it with anybody, I was trying constantly to put this in the background until I was getting rebellious. And I had a very bad temper. Now I usually could keep it under control, and I don't think anybody realized how I struggled with that internally. But I had this bad temper that was just really to me a bane."

Thus, when the "pressure of the Holy Spirit" was upon her, it made for much inner turmoil and bottled emotion. "We were having special meetings at church, and I was literally sick. I remember feeling badly because I kept the whole family home . . . and inwardly I knew it was the conviction of the Holy Spirit. So this is why I say to parents, don't underestimate how the Lord might be speaking to your children."

"I remember one time Mother saying, 'Geneva, don't you think it's time that you gave your heart to the Lord?' and I said, 'I don't think I'm so bad.' I think I had more spankings than all of the other kids put together, because I was always getting into things. But I knew when I said that, that boy, if there was anybody who needed to give her heart to the Lord, it was me."

One Sunday during an altar call at a communion service, Geneva went forward. By that time, she not only had decided to commit her life to Christ, but had mapped out how she was going to do it. Geneva greatly admired an aunt who had finished nurses' training and had decided to follow in her steps.

"I felt that in being a missionary, I either needed to choose teaching or nursing as a woman at that point, in order to go on the field and have a definite role. I chose nursing."

She focused on that goal from then on. In high school, she took courses with an eye to meeting prerequisites for nurses' training. But she kept her goal to herself in case she failed.

Several years later, however, Geneva learned that while she hadn't let her parents in on her plans, they hadn't been left out, either. Her future had been a big part of their thoughts and prayers.

She explains with these words:

"Although I hadn't shared with my parents my sense of call to the mission field, when my time of graduation from nurses' training was nearing, I got a letter from Mother. I don't know if I still have that letter, but her question went something like this: 'Geneva, we are just wondering what you plan to do with your life. How do you plan to use your nurses' training?' It was simply put.

"Now it was time to share with my parents. I wrote back and told them that I felt led to go to the mission field but didn't want to make any announcements about it until I saw I was really moving in that direction. I had heard several young people announce that they were going to the mission field, but it never materialized. I didn't want to add to their ranks.

"It didn't take many days for me to hear Mother's response. She said, 'I always felt that was what you were planning to do, but I wanted to hear it from you. Now I can tell you that before you were born, we told the Lord that if He wanted to use you in His service, we would be happy to give you into His hands. I didn't want to tell you until you made your decisions because I didn't want to influence you.'

"Mother was a wise woman and knew the call needed to be from God. Dad was not very vocal, but I knew he was one at heart with her. I don't know if the folks prayed that for each of us kids, but three out of four went to the mission field, and the fourth was called to stay at home, where he still does a great work for the Lord.

"The folks never stood in the way for our returning to the field, even when I'm sure they wondered if it was wise during times of political trouble. We have really appreciated my parent's submission to the Lord in all these things."

Other vital lessons Geneva learned in her childhood include:

- Don't confuse the circumstances you are born into as the determiner of your destiny.
- The fruit of the Spirit — faith, hope, love — make life sweet and significant. Possessions do not. So given the choice, the wise pursue the fruit of the Spirit.
- We succeed at life one day at a time, one small decision at a time. If those decisions are based on Godly principles, we will be building a foundation stronger that we can com- prehend at the time.
- Seek God's plan for your life. Don't expect it to be difficult to recognize.

The Noren family about 1945. In front are Amanda and David. Back, from left, are Evelyn, Willard, Edwin and Geneva.

Love And Trust

A Vignette

Her train from McCook, Neb., for Chicago pulled away from the station on the night of Aug. 5, 1949. Geneva was wracked with conflicting emotion. So much had happened, so quickly! She knew she was doing the will of God, yet if so, why did she feel so torn in her heart?

This was the wedding day of her younger brother, Willard. It had been a beautiful wedding, a wonderful time of reunion for her and her family, and yet, in many ways, a time of goodbyes as well. After the ceremony in the church she had grown up in, she had returned home to gather her bags to depart for the mission field in the Belgian Congo. She was 23, and it felt like she would never be home again.

She had seen this day coming since her childhood, although the details had not turned out as she had expected. First, she had always planned to serve in China, the mission field of special interest to her church, the Evangelical Covenant Church of America. Second, she had prepared herself emotionally to answer the call she had heard long ago, no matter what it meant to her personally. Love, marriage and motherhood were optional, but missionary service for God was not. Being near her beloved family was optional, but service to God was not. She was a very focused and determined young woman, trained in the medical profession, toughened to hardship and mentally prepared to put her hand to the plow without looking back.

She could see how God had helped her reach this point; she had had reassurances along the way that she was on the right path. She had seen God reshape her thinking and redirect her steps in ways that surprised and brought comfort. For example, the day before she was asked to suspend her college work to fill an immediate need in Africa, she had felt an almost unbearable burden to pray. During those moments of prayer, she had restated her willingness to serve wherever she was needed, and not where or when she decided to serve. Looking back a day later, that prayer would seem supernaturally appropriate in its wording. It enabled her, when the question came if she would go, to answer without hesitation or doubt. It was uncanny.

However, just when everything was seeming so clear, a complication entered Geneva's life. As the semester was ending, a young man had started dating her, and though she didn't mean to, she fell in love with him.

When she had agreed to go on that first date, a group picnic, she never imagined it could launch a relationship. It was supposed to be only a nice afternoon out. But they hit it off, and this young seminary student who had impressed her during her years at North Park College was impressed with her as well. By the time the semester ended, they were very much in love with each other.

As she sat on the train that night, Aug. 5, 1949, she wondered. Did service to God mean she was going to have to not look back at him as well? This person who she realized was probably the only man she would ever want to marry?

Geneva had been placing this and other emotional questions before God in prayer. As she struggled with her feelings, she refused to even voice them to anyone in hopes that silence would help, or at least not distract from Willard's big day. But her sorrow was written all over her. Even Willard, busily preparing for his marriage, could sense inner turmoil in his sister. Why wouldn't it be there? For this seminary student from Washington had turned up at her little Kansas church, at the time of her brother's wedding, when she would still be there, to sing as a member of a trio at revival services that had been scheduled a year before! It was uncanny.

He was even at the rehearsal party the night before the wedding! And when Geneva left the party that night, her brother came out to the car with her and asked her about him.

Her emotions won over her stoic silence. She poured out her feelings to her brother. There had never been anyone like this man in her life. He truly was a man of God, and she loved him not only for what he was but because of the way he loved Christ. There would never be another like him in her life. And tomorrow she was leaving. Him. Her family. Everything she loved was being left behind, except the Lord.

Willard comforted and encouraged her, but as she drove away from the rehearsal party, she cried.

The next day was the wedding, and the love of her life was there. The ceremony was tender and emotional. The reception was festive. Then Geneva had to leave. Her bags were packed and waiting at her family's house, and she had to get ready for her train.

He walked up to her as she was leaving the reception at the church. Could he escort her to the train?

No, she said. She kept the reason to herself: Leaving him there would only hurt more than leaving him here, right now, quickly.

At the little farmhouse where she had grown up, her parents helped her gather her bags. What a day for her mother! she thought. A son married. A daughter going away, to return, if ever, who knew when.

Here was more turmoil for Geneva. Her family meant more to her than anything on earth. She felt very much for her mother and how this must be for her. But her mother and father, as well as Geneva, knew there was a call on her life, and today was the day.

Geneva's footsteps to the train had been prefaced with a lot of prayer about all these issues within her. She had determined, in prayer, that if this man was meant for her, God would see that they were brought together. No matter that her seminary student planned to serve in China. No matter that they were going to spend their lives serving on different continents. She knew God made all good things come to them who wait on Him. She knew she was supposed to be in Africa. And if her love for this man was right in God's eyes, He would save their relationship, and He would shape it as He willed, no matter the distance, no matter the form.

Geneva was trusting this to the Lord, as she had learned to do since childhood. He had always made a way before, even when it seemed there was no way. She'd seen it happen. So on Aug. 5, 1949, she trusted Him with everything she had in her heart.

She walked to the train. Her parents helped her get her bags aboard. She kissed them goodbye. She waved to them from the closed window. She watched them stand together on the platform as she pulled away from them.

Then she turned in her seat, her heart quivering. There was so much happening! There was so much turmoil inside...

As she sat there, she could feel a warm blanket being laid over her. It was so comforting. It brought such peace to her troubled mind. She closed her eyes. "It's all right," she could almost hear someone say. "I love you."

There was no warm blanket, really. Her soul was being comforted, so wonderfully that she could feel it with her body. Her mind relaxed, soothed. The turmoil left.

She would remember for the rest of her life that sensation of the Lord's presence with her on the train. It was so real, it was uncanny.

Gordon Christensen at North Park College, 1949.

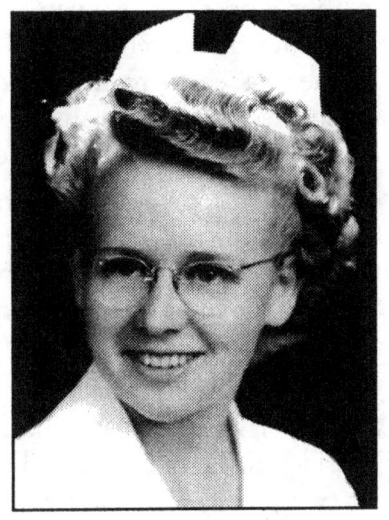

Geneva Noren before leaving for the mission field, 1949.

Chapter 3

A Romance at North Park

Geneva was too young to get into nursing school when she graduated from high school in 1943, so she went to work in Denver for nine months. She worked as a cook for the wealthy Werder family, owners of the Green Parrot restaurant chain, and then as a clerk in a shipping company. Finally, she couldn't wait any longer to start preparing to be a missionary nurse. A friend got her her first hospital job, at Children's Memorial Hospital.

Geneva worked in the surgery department preparing sterile packs and doing cleanup. The experience was fantastic for her, and she was even allowed to scrub up and attend some surgical procedures. She was a young person with a goal, so she was eager to learn more and do more, because she recognized that it was all preparation for her life's work. She knew what she was trying to do.

After about seven months at Children's Memorial, Geneva returned home to spend several months with her family before starting an intensive training program at Swedish Covenant Hospital in Chicago. It was autumn 1944, and she was now of age, 18 1/2.

Geneva did not have the money to pay for training, but the government was in such need of nurses for service in World War II that it offered to pay for training in exchange for two years' service in a military hospital. If the war ended before the nursing student was trained, she was released from the obligation of the Nurses Cadet Program.

Geneva was torn about enrolling. She questioned whether it would be right to delay her start on the mission field to fulfill the two years of service as a military nurse.

"This was a real problem for me, because I wanted to go to the mission field as soon as I could," she said. "But I really had no choice. I knew if I borrowed the money, I would still be stuck at home having to pay that back."

She finally decided to enroll in the program and began her training.

The workload was tremendous. With many of the nation's professional nurses already serving in the war effort, the young trainees found that keeping the Chicago hospital afloat depended largely on them.

"We really worked," Geneva said. "It was not an easy program. You lived, ate, slept right in the dormitories of the hospital, and you worked until the work was finished." On top of that was formal classroom training.

"The whole hospital was run by student nurses except for several supervisory positions. On weekends, even most of those supervisory jobs were run by senior students. So that meant sometimes we worked very long days. ... But that too was excellent training for the mission field, because I got experience in things that today no one gets in nurses training programs. So it was all very good. I could see where the Lord blessed in that situation."

Geneva's year-round training lasted for three years, until 1947. Victory in Japan had been declared in late 1945, so nurse-trainee Geneva Noren — along with most of her classmates — became military surplus from the war. When she finished her training program, she was free to go.

However, another obstacle had appeared in Geneva's horizon. The Covenant Church had advised her to get some formal Bible study at North Park College, its liberal arts school and seminary in Chicago, before going onto the field. Geneva agreed to the delay, in great part because it would allow her something she sorely missed — some more time with her family. Upon graduation from nurses training in the fall, she went home to spend the winter with her family before starting in North Park in September. It became a very important summer for the entire Noren family.

Geneva was working at the hospital in Oberlin and living in town, but she attended a church camp at Covenant Heights, a facility opening that year outside Denver. The church had almost called off the event, because Covenant Heights wasn't finished. The project had been prayed over a great deal, and members decided to proceed anyway, saying, "We're going to do it, so pray a lot, and the Lord will bless." Harvey Widman was the missionary who served as speaker, and the Rev. Edwin Johnson, who was a capable guitar player, served as Bible teacher. Geneva served as camp nurse.

In those days such events were not as segregated by age as they are currently. So this "young peoples' camp" included teenagers, college students, even young married couples. Thus, there was a large delegation from Geneva's church, including her sister, Evelyn.

"From the time we hit those grounds, there was an unusual presence of God that I had never experienced before," Geneva recalled. "That camp was the camp that turned our church around spiritually, really, and a lot of other churches."

The camp's dining room, fellowship hall and tabernacle were all unfinished. Yet the people who attended seemed to add the vital finishing touch, a powerful spirit of personal rededication.

"At the front of the tabernacle, they had built a kind of riser," Geneva said. "Every night, there were just puddles of tears. Literally puddles of tears. And I've reminded people of that. I said, 'This floor, this area is sacred.' It was baptized with the tears of people my age, some a little younger, some a little older. People were saved, and many made meaningful commitments to the Lord. There had been a lot of on-the-fence Christians in our church and other churches. But that camp was the time when they became meaningful followers of the Lord. ... You would go up there afterward, and there were just wet spots where young people had been weeping out to the Lord. The spirit of God was magnificent. And the speakers I can remember, because I sat on the front row. I was drinking this in. And it was at this time that the Lord spoke to me.

"I had been telling Him where I was going to go as a missionary. That was China. I had gone through all the statistics, and China was the nation that needed the Gospel more, per capita. I said, 'Never to Africa. They've got more missionaries than anybody else.' And that's when the Lord got hold of me and made me realize that I was dictating to Him and not listening to Him.

"If the Lord had not gotten through to me at that time, I might never have gotten to the mission field."

Less than one year after that camp — and the very year Geneva started missionary work — the communist takeover of China closed the nation completely to missionaries. The time of sowing by foreign missionaries was over. The mission field that had actually inspired the formation of the Evangelical Covenant Church of America and had been its main focus since the late 1800s was now cut off from the Christian church worldwide. The infant church started in China would now have to survive decades of persecution on the grace of God alone.

Before that time began, however, Geneva realized that she was being presumptuous about where she would serve, and that realization began to prepare her mentally for a change in direction. She says that the reason it was so important to correct her thinking then was that she could have easily mistaken the closing of China as a signal that she had not really been called as a missionary. Instead, during that dynamic church camp of 1948, it dawned on her profoundly that she had only been called to serve; she had not yet been told where to serve.

Geneva's sister, Evelyn, also was affected profoundly during that week-long church camp.

The two sisters were sleeping in bunks, Evelyn below, Geneva above. One night, Evelyn woke Geneva up with the question, "What do you want?"

"I don't want anything. I'm sleeping," Geneva told her.

"You called me."

"No, I didn't call you."

There was silence in the cabin, but a little while later Evelyn woke Geneva up again.

"What do you want?"

Geneva was getting exasperated. "I don't want anything. Evelyn, I am trying to sleep!"

"But I heard my name."

Geneva began to think. She went back to sleep, and sure enough, Evelyn woke her up a third time, saying she had heard her name. Geneva and Evelyn realized that the Lord was calling her. "She began to realize that the Lord called

Samuel with an audible voice. She felt, 'I don't know who I am that He would call me, but He might be calling me.' And that's when she said, 'Yes Lord, I'll go where you want me to go.'"

Evelyn soon felt that call was to the mission field, even though she was already employed as a teacher and had a teaching contract yet to fulfill.

When Evelyn returned to school to begin the new year, she told the principal that she felt called to service as a missionary. But class assignments were already made and she was needed at the school. "If you can find a replacement, you go with my blessing," the principal told her.

As Evelyn stepped out of his office, there stood an old classmate of hers. "Do you think there's any chance of my getting a teaching job this late in the game? I'm desperate for a job."

Evelyn turned around and walked back into the principal's office. "Here is my replacement," she announced. It had taken less than a minute to find her, and the woman taught at the school the rest of her life.

Evelyn then joined Geneva and her oldest brother, Ed, as a student at North Park College.

When Geneva and Evelyn began classes in the fall of 1948, Geneva already knew who Gordon Christensen was. Gordon and his friend Glen Wiberg had visited the Oberlin area doing evangelistic work in 1946. They spent a week helping with summer Bible school and having church meetings in the evenings. Although she was in the nurses training program at Swedish Covenant Hospital, Geneva heard about Gordon when she returned for a brief visit. Her aunt Maude Holmdahl told her about the nice young man from North Park who had visited that summer. "He would be a really nice young man for you," she told Geneva.

Geneva wasn't interested at all. She was busy with her training and did not have time for anything else.

In 1947, Gordon was back in Oberlin during the summer and stayed with another aunt and uncle of Geneva's. Thus, the Noren family was well acquainted with Gordon Christensen before Geneva had met him.

The talk about this man in Oberlin, however, did not escape Geneva's attention completely. When she arrived at North Park for her Bible training, she was curious about Gordon and watched for him.

It didn't take very long to find Gordon. He was the leader of a campus group called Missionary Volunteers, which held prayer meetings at 10 a.m. every Tuesday. It was the biggest organization on campus at the time and focused on praying for missionaries and missionary needs.

As a newcomer to the campus, Geneva noticed Gordon right away — because of the power of his words. She first heard Gordon when he gave a Wednesday night chapel message.

"When I went to North Park, and I heard him preach, it was his preaching that really attracted me," Geneva said. "There was more life and spirit in his preaching than many of the students who would give their messages. So I knew who he was, and I saw him around school, but we never paid any attention to each other."

She was not exactly right on that count. Gordon HAD noticed her, but not by sight. At a Missionary Volunteers meeting, he heard a woman he did not know begin to pray with such strength, that after the meeting, he asked a friend, who was that?

"That's Ed Noren's sister, Geneva," was the answer.

Years later, Gordon recalled, "There was a fervency about the prayer, and I felt anyone who could pray that well ought to be on my team."

Thus, her presence on the North Park campus was duly noted by the leader of the Missionary Volunteers, but no personal relationship began at that time. Geneva was busy getting through Bible study as quickly as possible so she could get to the mission field, and Gordon was busy with his studies in the seminary.

Before she ever recognized it, Geneva came to a major turning point in her life. The day arrived for a crucial decision, though unbeknown to her, and the principles for living that had been taught to her and modeled for her would now be put into play and determine the outcome.

It was after the 1949 midwinter conference — the annual denominational meeting for the Evangelical Covenant Church — that Geneva, her sister Evelyn and several other friends decided to go for a walk. It was a snowy January afternoon in Chicago when they set out for some fresh air. During that walk, Geneva began to feel she needed to pray. Something had to be dealt with, but she didn't know what. Geneva describes the day this way:

"I got a heavy burden on my heart. I didn't know what it was. I was trying to think, was somebody sick? What's the problem? I didn't realize I was facing a crisis, and I excused myself. I said I felt like I needed to go home a little bit.

"I went back to our little basement apartment where two other girls and I lived. And I went to prayer. I said to the Lord, 'I have NO idea what this burden is on my heart.' But I restated to the Lord — it seemed like the Lord guided me to restate my goals and preparation and commitment to Him for whatever He had, and my goal was still the mission field and so forth.

"I restated all of these things to the Lord and my willingness to go out, because at this point I had worked out this whole thing about being single, and again I said I will go as a single person and I will be happy, because my happiness will come from You and not people. I kind of went through a reaffirmation like this, and it didn't take long at all.

"All of a sudden, the burden lifted. ... I felt tremendous joy, and I went out and joined these friends walking again. I don't think they had gotten all that far if I could catch up with them, you know. I'm sure they wondered what my ailment was."

Geneva didn't know either, until the next day.

As she was leaving his class that day, the professor of missions, Dr. Fondell, asked Geneva if he could speak with her about something important.

There was a need on the African mission field now. World War II had made it difficult to get medical personnel to the missionaries. Making matters worse, the war had prevented the mission board from getting missionaries in or out of Africa, so exhausted missionaries could not get furloughs for rest or recuperation. Sickness was rampant, and there was only one doctor and one nurse on the field to handle it all. Would she be willing to end her formal Bible training and go to the mission field earlier than planned? Even now?

The answer was simple. She practically shouted "Yes!"

Geneva says the reason for that sudden burden during a winter's walk had become apparent within 24 hours:

"I realized then that God just needed me to reaffirm my commitments to Him before getting this word, so that I wasn't going to go through this muddle ... to reaffirm so that when this calling came, 'there's a place open for you,' that without hesitation I would go."

The moment had come that Geneva had known would come since she was 12 years old. The preparation was ending. The mission board had decided she would finish the semester, get her affairs in order during the summer and leave for Africa in the fall. Her course was set.

Or was it? There was another complication about to enter her life that could alter her route: romance.

In 1949 Gordon Christensen was serving as associate pastor for the Portage Park Covenant Church in the north end of Chicago. The pastor was the Rev. Kenneth Swanson. Gordon helped him with duties such as visiting the sick, and he also led the choir, although years later he would say that his title "associate pastor" glorified his contribution a bit.

That winter, the Rev. Swanson's wife was dying of cancer. As death approached, Geneva Noren was asked to spend what was expected to be Mrs. Swanson's last night as her nurse on duty.

"It was a long and difficult night," she said. "She would not take any medication. She is a woman I learned a lot from in her last night on this earth, because never did she talk about her own pain. She wanted to know what I was going to do with my life, and so forth.

"She died the next morning, shortly after I had gone off duty."

It was yet another time of reaffirmation for Geneva as once again she reviewed her own priorities and goals.

Because he had been so closely associated with the pastor, his family and church, Gordon wanted to attend the viewing at the mortuary. Gordon's good friend Gordon Johnson, who would go on to spend 30 years as a missionary in Japan, was the only person he knew with a car, so he got Gordon Johnson to give him a ride.

As they came out of North Park College and were turning onto Foster Avenue, there stood Geneva and Evelyn, waiting for a bus to take them to the viewing. Gordon Johnson stopped and asked them if they needed a ride. The two women said yes, saved the bus fare, and launched a romance.

"My brother-in-law, telling about this on our 25th wedding anniversary, said, 'they met in a morgue,'" Gordon recalled with a laugh. "Which was not true. I pled with him, 'Don't say that. Say that we met on our way down to a mortuary to a viewing.' He said, 'No. You met in a morgue. I'm going to tell it my way.'"

Though they started a personal relationship under peculiar circumstances, the relationship started nonetheless. Gordon asked Geneva on their first date for a Memorial Day outing, May 30, 1949.

"I felt very safe going out with anybody, because my course was set," Geneva said. "I was on my way to the mission field. I was going to be leaving in August, and I had had this whole thing out with the Lord. I wanted to go as a single person, because the single ladies had told me they were the ones that got the work done — the men and single ladies. I wanted to get the work done. But I said to the Lord, 'I want to be a happy single person. I don't want to go out there grumbling because I'm single. ... I had prayed through this whole thing and come to a real victory in the whole matter. So when he asked me to go out, I thought, 'No problem,' because I had this decision made with the Lord.

"So I went out with him, thinking this was just a little outing. I needed an outing; we were taking final exams. I went out with him, not realizing what a trouble it was going to be in my heart for a while."

The date was a picnic sponsored by the men in Gordon's dormitory, Hjerpe House, where the single male seminary students lived. About eight to ten men and their dates headed out for what Gordon says was a park, but what Geneva describes as a cow pasture.

They had a wonderful time, and Gordon found himself more and more impressed with Geneva Noren. Days later he asked her to the big event at North Park College, the choir presentation in Orchestra Hall in downtown Chicago. When the day arrived about two weeks after their Memorial Day picnic, Gordon was ready: He had gotten hold of a brand new car he was asked to ferry to the West Coast for a motor company, so he had a nice set of wheels for the big night. It was another great time.

Gordon was in love.

The men in Gordon's dorm decided they would help Cupid along. They started telling Geneva how smitten Gordon was for her.

"The last few days we had left of school, they were having a good time," Geneva says. "They would surround me and tell me what a fit he was having back there in the dormitory! They said he was pacing the floor, saying, 'Where have I been? Why didn't I see her before?' All this kind of thing. They had a lot of fun with that.

"I was still headed for the mission field, but I realized when I had gone out with him, well, I had never been out with anybody I felt such a kinship of spirit with before. And I thought, 'Oh Lord, why in the world did I go out with him?' I had all this settled and now I had to go back to the drawing board and start praying through this whole thing again. Because I thought if I ever did marry, that would be the man I would marry."

She realized Gordon planned to go to China, but now she was going in the opposite direction, to Africa, as it had seemed was God's will. If she was not careful with this relationship, what if Gordon ignored God's calling to serve Him in China because of her?

"I certainly wouldn't want anyone to go to Africa because I was there," Geneva says. "It would have to be their own calling. So I prayed, and the Lord gave me Psalm 84:"

> *For the Lord God is a sun and shield: the Lord will give grace and glory: no good thing will he withhold from them that walk uprightly. O Lord of hosts, blessed is the man that trusteth in thee.*

"I thought, 'Lord, that's it. If I walk uprightly and Gordon's a good thing for me, you will not withhold him, no matter where our sights are set at this time.'

"So I left it like that with the Lord. But it made it very difficult, because of how I felt at this point, and as I said, his classmates were very willing to let me know how he was feeling. But he never said anything, realizing I was in a real tight squeeze of time, getting ready to go to the field, and it wasn't really fair to start talking about how he felt about our time together."

Geneva finished her courses and headed home for about a month before it was time to leave for Africa. Her brother Willard was getting married Aug. 5, 1949, the same day she was to board the train for New York City and take a freighter to Africa.

It was a stressful time for Geneva. She had always been close to her family, and this mission to Africa had such a sense of permanence to her, it seemed to her as if these were final farewells. Of course, there would be furloughs and visits, but the days of living as a family — of trips to the fishing hole, Sunday afternoon baseball, family devotionals — were about to end.

On top of that, there was a tug on her heart that she was leaving behind the man she realized she loved.

She was answering the call she had felt on her life ever since childhood, but in this month, it suddenly seemed that it would be harder to answer with, "Here I am, send me."

There was yet another surprise coming for that summer: as the Lord would have it, Gordon's summer itinerary for evangelism put him at the Noren family's church during Geneva's last week home. Gordon said years later in an interview that it was not by his design; the itinerary had been established months before. But he certainly appreciated the chance to see Geneva again.

Gordon arrived at Herndon Covenant Church as part of a musical trio that included fellow North Park students Gordon Johnson and Dick "Butch" Reynolds. They had put on weeklong evangelistic meetings at Covenant churches across the Midwest with Gordon playing the trumpet, Butch playing piano and Gordon Johnson singing with Gordon and taking his turn at preaching.

The evening meetings were full of music and preaching. Gordon was then and still is a powerful speaker with a gift for building enthusiasm and vision. Trips such as these were times of great spiritual growth for him that would become essential to his ministry for the rest of his life. It seems God was laying a foundation in Gordon's life on such evangelistic trips that would become more and more evident in years to come. But on this trip, there was a special personal interest as well. Geneva attended the special evening services, and once again was seeing why she loved this man so much.

"To have him and these two other fellows there at that time didn't make my leaving home any easier," she said. "Even though I had put this in the Lord's hands, to have him around — I still had this sense, this real oneness of spirit with him."

She and Gordon never talked about it during that week. "I thought, 'God has to be first, He WILL be first, and I have

Gordon, left, and Glen Wiberg go fishing in Kansas about 1945.

left this in the Lord's hands. So now I don't say anything about this to anybody."

However, Geneva was not successful in completely concealing her feelings. On the evening of Aug. 4, 1949, her brother Willard came out of his rehearsal party to talk to Geneva about this man Gordon.

"I remember I was out in the car after practice, and I was ready to go home because I was getting very tired. I had done a lot of things in preparation for going to the field," she said.

But Willard asked her about Gordon, and she told him how she felt. She also said that it was committed to the Lord, though the opportunity to voice her feelings, and to voice again her commitment, was very helpful to her.

The next day, Saturday, was the wedding. Everyone from the church was invited, and Gordon and his two friends also came. Willard's and Geneva's older brother, Edwin, the North Park seminary student, performed the service.

But it was the reception afterward, in the basement of the Herndon Covenant Church, that touched Gordon the most. The festivities stopped, and Willard gave his Christian testimony. He spoke of how this marriage would be built on a love for the Lord and the teachings of the Bible. How he wanted this marriage to be to the glory of the Lord.

"I will never forget that wedding," Gordon says. "It was the only wedding I had seen up to this point where the groom stood up and gave a personal testimony of his faith in Christ and how he was committing this marriage to the Lord, and he wanted everybody to know it. It was marvelous."

It was also good, Geneva says, because Willard at 21 and his bride, Esther Benda, at 19, were considered too young by many to be getting married, and there were some dire predictions about how this union was going to work out. "Well, Willard's and Esther's marriage has been one of the biggest testimonies, I'd say, in the whole community," Geneva says.

With the wedding over, Geneva had to gather her bags and go to the train station. Her mind was flooded with conflicting thoughts and emotions. One of the foremost thoughts was the impact this day must be having on her mother. Her youngest son was getting married, and her daughter was leaving for the mission field in Africa.

As the wedding reception was winding down and Geneva was leaving, Gordon walked up to her. Could he see her to the train station and say goodbye there?

She looked at him for a moment. Here were more emotions for her to struggle with on that important day.

"I said 'No. You've come for special meetings here; you stay and do your meetings and I'll go to the train with my folks.' It was very difficult. I shook hands with him there, told him goodbye, had no idea how this would ever work out. But it was in God's hands."

She rushed home and changed her clothes, then left for the train station. She was very concerned, on top of everything else, about how her mother would be taking this day.

"A 23-year-old does not look real old when you think of them traveling by themselves that distance. But I was very confident that the Lord had gone before, and I knew He had, and they knew that too, but I knew the stress on Mom that day had to be awful.

"I had prayed, because as I said before, my family was so important, and I knew leaving for that length of time would really be hard. And I prayed, 'Oh Lord, just do something special, especially for the folks in that hour, too. They were tired.

"And when I got on that train, I could feel, literally feel, something like a warm blanket being put around me. I don't know if I have ever had that much of a sensation of God's presence — you know He comes in different ways, but to me that was such a blessing that it just took away the stress of that hour."

LIFE LESSONS

Throughout her life, even in her youth, Geneva has measured circumstances by the Word of God. It is a standard she saw modeled by her family, and one she continued to exercise in her personal decisions, both large and small. What does the Word of God have to say about this? Is there a principle to consider instead of the example of friends or popular culture? Is it wrong or not, according to the standards God set?

"When I came to any crisis situation, I went to the scriptures to look for God's guidance in it."

This was her scale for making decisions, notably at this point in her life when she decided that God was calling her to the mission field early, and then when she could trust her personal relationship with Gordon in the Lord's hands.

Today, at the turn of the century, when in America personal fulfillment is touted as the most important goal, Geneva's decision to risk her personal relationship with Gordon is a shock to many of the young people she meets.

"I've told this sometimes to young people, and they can't imagine that," she says. "But I say, 'You know, when you dare to commit something to the Lord, He will work it out. You don't have to be trying to help Him.' So I think it was good the way the Lord enabled us at that time."

It was another step in faith, one of many that already had been taken. And Geneva says it is only by taking those steps one at a time, that when we finally reach the important junctures in our lives, we are prepared to follow the guidance that already has been proven. Our walks with Christ will begin much like our walks in the world began, with tiny steps, small advancements, but with the persistence and enthusiasm of a toddler who has so much to gain by improving this skill. If we continue, the day can come when we are walking in the confidence of God's promises as if He had personally guaranteed them to us. For He has, in both word and deed:

> "For thou art my lamp, O Lord: and the Lord will lighten my darkness. For by thee I have run through a troop: by my God have I leaped over a wall. As for God, his way is perfect: he is a buckler (shield) to all them that trust in him. For who is God, save the Lord? and who is a rock, save our God? God is my strength and power: and he maketh my way perfect. He maketh my feet like hinds' feet: and setteth me upon my high places." — 2 Samuel 22:29-34

Just as the small mountain deer, the hind, was so admired for its surefootedness at the world's most precarious heights, so can people be spiritually surefooted and travel to the greatest heights of life with confidence — the supernatural confidence that comes from a relationship with the King of Kings, Jesus Christ.

Geneva boards her freighter en route to the Congo, August 11, 1949.

Chapter 4

Off to Africa

With a mission as noble as Geneva Noren's, you would think she would be permitted to avoid some of the more earthy problems of life. But she wasn't.

She left New York Harbor on a Belgian freighter, one of the "Liberty ships" that had been cranked out as part of the war effort. Her destination: the port city of Matadi, Belgian Congo, Africa.

With her was a mountain of supplies that had been gathered for the mission field, including two vehicles. Though she could speak little French, and she was responsible for these supplies for a new mission station, "I had such faith at the time, it didn't bother me a bit," she says.

One of the problems was being a young single girl alone on a ship with a bunch of aggressive merchant seaman — and a captain who was worse than them all.

"Talk about a bunch of vultures!" Geneva says. "Those sailors had been out there at sea like that. My mother had given me good teaching, and I learned to get a pretty thick skin on my nose that trip."

God gave her some help in the form of a 6-year-old boy named Bobby. He was the son of a Baptist missionary couple also on their way to Africa. Geneva and Bobby went everywhere together on the ship. Geneva would go to the bow and practice on her accordion — a gift from her youth group — that she had to learn to play. Bobby stuck with her through it all, and his parents were glad to have another adult watching over their son.

But vultures can be hard to deter. Eventually the captain's steward came to Geneva with an invitation for tea in the captain's cabin. She told the steward absolutely not. The invitation became more forceful, so Geneva offered a compromise. She would come to tea if Bobby could come with her. That was accepted, but Geneva says she got in and out of there as quickly as she could. She had a feeling the captain was "no good."

She was right. When the ship crossed the equator, the crew and passengers kept the tradition of having a Neptune initiation feast. The captain got a little drunk, much to the discomfort of the passengers.

Geneva was sitting between the captain and the first mate, and the captain, she says, "got a little too friendly."

Geneva decided it was time to make herself clear. She threw a glass of quinine water on him. He left enraged, and to Geneva's surprise, other missionaries were embarrassed.

Her response: "None of you stood up and said, 'Look, Mr. Captain, that's enough.' Or, 'Could she please come sit with us?' None of you made a move. I took things into my own hands, whether you like it or not."

She adds, "I don't think he came down for another meal while I was on the boat.

"I never felt like apologizing to anybody because my moral standards were set, and nobody was going to act like that around me. So I caused the missionaries a little embarrassment."

There was another misadventure on the trip, however; one that was much more dangerous.

Several days into the trip, in the middle of the journey, Geneva was summoned for a medical problem. A cabin boy had become sick.

The young man appeared to have appendicitis and was so sick that Geneva was afraid his appendix would burst. His temperature was soaring.

Geneva had him packed in ice and gave him some antibiotics. But he was in serious trouble. The first mate then asked her if she could operate on him and remove his appendix.

"Oh Lord," she thought. "Here I go, over my head again."

She went back to her cabin and prayed. She had been in enough surgery to feel that it was possible.

"Today that consideration would be ridiculous, but at that moment, it was something to consider."

She asked to see their supplies. She said she never would do it unless it was absolutely necessary, and if they could contact another ship with a doctor aboard who would take responsibility for it; a huge responsibility on a doctor who had no idea who Geneva Noren was.

Geneva went back to her cabin and prayed hard. This had to be more than she could do, but if she denied that boy a skill or knowledge that might save him, that would be wrong, too. Which way to turn?

"As He had done so many times, God delivered me — and He delivered that boy," Geneva says. "The infection subsided until we could get him to port in Matadi and then put him on a faster ship and get him to Brussels. He had surgery there. Boy, those were tense moments."

When she got to Matadi, she was greeted by a Mr. Waltander of the Swedish Mission. She had expected to be lodged in a guest house, but it was so full with missionaries unable to get out of the country, because boats had not been coming, that she could not stay there. Mr. Waltander said she and all missionaries would have to lodge on the ship — unless there was somebody there on board could speak Swedish. There were many Americans at the missionary lodging house, and his wife could not speak English. Geneva was allowed to leave the ship, and she took another young woman with her who was desperate to get off the ship.

"I was able to help Mrs. Waltander, and then Mr. Waltander was able to help me," Geneva says. "See how the Lord provided? I had this big shipment with me, all these invoices, and I couldn't even speak French. Mr. Waltander said, 'That's all right, you help mama here, and I'll help you get through customs."

Mr. Waltander got her a sun helmet and made her wear it. "He was just like an old papa," Geneva says.

He was fluent in many languages, and he knew how the system worked. Geneva suddenly learned that she was supposed to know the value — and the French names — of all the materials she had brought for the mission! The thought froze her, but not Mr. Waltander. He put down the prices he knew — and guessed at the rest.

It took 10 days to get the material through customs, even with Mr. Waltander's help.

"The Lord provided for me," Geneva says. "I was so ignorant. It was just terrible how ignorant I was, and the Lord just provided everything."

Finally, the customs hurdle was crossed, and Mr. Waltander helped Geneva get a driver's license for the Belgian Congo.

She had been in Matadi two weeks getting paperwork in order. Then she set out on a two-day drive through the bush to Leopoldville, where she then took a plane for Lisala while the supplies were shipped by boat. Geneva had sent telegrams ahead saying when she would arrive, but when she reached Lisala, there was no one there to meet her.

An American man who had ridden on the plane asked where her friends were. When she said no one was meeting her, he left for a few minutes and came back with a man in a uniform. He would take her to the Baptist mission, he said, then he boarded his flight and was gone.

The man drove Geneva to the mission, where she found Helen Price and Orville Davis from the Covenant Church's mission. Orville had brought Helen to the river port of Lisala to catch a riverboat to Coquilhatville, where the Disciples of Christ had a mission. Helen was going to be teaching high school, a job several missions teamed up to accomplish.

As the man was leaving, Geneva asked him how much she owed him. She thought he was a taxi driver. The man stiffened. So did Helen Price. Geneva thought to herself, 'What's wrong with these people?'

As the man drove off, Helen told her, "Wave to him!"

"I just don't wave to everybody," Geneva protested.

But the man wasn't an "everybody"; he was the governor of the province! How the man Geneva met on the airplane ever got such a favor from such a high official, she never knew. But to cover for the faux pas, Helen later wrote him a very nice letter and made Geneva sign it.

A grueling drive began to the mission station in Gbado and later, Karawa. The journey was so rough that Geneva remembers tie rods breaking on the rutted roads. To keep the truck running, the tie rods were lashed together with vines cut from the side of the road.

When Geneva finally reached Karawa, she found the missionaries sick and a hospital with one doctor and one nurse.

Much of her ministry for the first year was caring for those sick missionaries.

When she reached the mission field, she had to hit the ground running, and the pace never let up. She would get up each morning at 4:30 for private devotions, then self-study in language. At 6 a.m. was a mission chapel service, then the day began in earnest. The workload was intense.

One of the lessons Geneva learned in those days was how hard the married women on the field worked. They not only raised their own families but did everything else that might fall through the cracks as others carried out more formal assignments. She realized the stories of married women not being involved in the work were the result of poor observation. Those women were deeply involved, but they did not get the credit. And it dawned on Geneva that if it were her, such nonrecognition would be very hard to endure.

Folks at the mission began to notice all the letters coming to Geneva from a Gordon Christensen at North Park College.

They were love letters, but not traditionally romantic. Gordon relied on romantic sounding Bible verses to communicate his feelings, such as 3 John 2: "Beloved, I wish above all things that thou mayest prosper and be in health, even as thy soul prospereth."

He laughs now that the reason he used that verse in one letter was because it had a very telling word in it — "Beloved" — yet Geneva says the letters, full of scripture and encouragement, were a lifeline to her. They kept her going and helped keep her from being overwhelmed with the daunting task before her. "We gave each other a lot of scripture, but that's really what I existed on."

Finally Gordon sent her a letter with the big question: "I'm just wondering if you'd like to change your name to Christensen."

The letter arrived in Geneva's hands on her birthday.

At the time she had been caring for an entire missionary family that was sick. The mother, who had lost a baby in delivery, had sunk into a severe depression and required almost constant care. Yet Geneva also had the father and children to care for. This strain had gone on for a couple of weeks. Geneva could barely get enough free time to eat a meal. When she got the letter, she put it in her pocket without opening it.

Late that night she had the family down for sleep. She was staying on a cot in the woman's room. Just before she went to bed, she opened the letter.

Gordon's proposal did not take her by surprise. She had been praying about her relationship with him. The sticking point for her was whether she would be willing to live life without being recognized as a missionary in her own right. Was she willing instead to be a missionary wife, a person whose contribution might often be overlooked?

LIFE LESSONS

Geneva found that no amount of preparation can ever take the place of trust in God. Years of nurse's training could not become her primary source of strength. No matter how much a person prepares for his chosen mission in life, his own strength, intelligence or calmness under pressure will not be sufficient for all challenges. Such strength of self is in the realm of fiction: it is found in James Bonds or Rambos. For people in the real world, there are too many potential opponents.

> *"For we wrestle not against flesh and blood, but against principalities, against powers, against the rulers of the darkness of this world, against spiritual wickedness in high places."* — Ephesians 6:12

That is why the competition can easily outstrip whatever natural ability or training a person may possess. And of particular interest to those challengers are the people who choose to live in service to God. For everyone — and especially for those focused on living for Him — the only hope is to know God, understand His word and ways, and be willing to follow Him.

Doctors need faith in God to be the greatest doctors they can be. Young people need faith in God in order to find fulfilling dreams. Missionary workers need to keep refueling their faith in God in order not to be overwhelmed by the needs of the world.

The strength to run the entire race can only come from God. If we recognize that, Geneva says, we can be more than conquerors through Him who loves us.

Facing Unknowns

A Vignette

Geneva walked toward the grass hut with the dose of antibiotics that the new patient needed. She had never seen this man who had been brought to the Karawa Mission Station after being seriously injured by a buffalo. But the African nurses on the station shied away from treating him and the staff doctor had asked her to take him the medicine.

Sure, she said, why not? But why won't the Africans?

She was told simply, "They won't go in the hut."

Geneva had been on the mission field only about five months on this January day in 1950, but she had years of experience by then. Work at hospitals in the U.S. where she had been allowed to scrub up and stand by in surgical operations had braced her for just about anything.

But she wasn't prepared for this. When she stooped down and entered the grass hut, she instinctively recoiled at what she saw. She nearly backed out of the hut again.

It wasn't gore that stunned her, although the man had had a gory wound; the people who had brought him to the mission station said the buffalo had ripped his abdomen open and disemboweled him.

It was his eyes. There was something horrific in his gaze.

The man's entrails were back in his body, and on his abdomen was a long, jagged scar. But on his thigh was an identical wound, deep and ghastly, unhealed.

She gave him the medicine and quickly left the hut, and went to get some answers.

The African nurses told her that the man was a village witch doctor, and that he said when he arrived at the station earlier that day that he had used his power to transfer the wound. He was known to be able to transfer people as well, using his magic to instantaneously transport people to villages miles away.

Geneva and her fellow missionary nurse, Maxine, didn't know what to do with the man. They talked to a newly arrived missionary pastor and asked him to at least go talk to the man, because here was a soul that, if the man died, was doomed to damnation.

The missionary pastor did go, and he did pray for the man, but the man refused to pray for salvation, or for himself, or to accept the Christian message.

The man died shortly thereafter, and Geneva was never able to forget him. For one thing, he was her first encounter with a fearfully evil power. He personified what she had once dismissed as superstition. Also, she realized that, given her penchant for preparation, preparation, preparation, she was not prepared at all to face this sort of thing. How could it be real if it was so unheard of?

She had neatly categorized the weird tales of witch doctors, evil spirits and the supernatural as the explanations conjured up by uneducated people. And maybe, somehow, this transferrance of wound was some sort of lie, too, although, if it was, it was a very good one. But if she stuck to her original reasoning, she could catalog this episode with other unexplainables and put it away.

But she could not. Because it wasn't the wound that alarmed her. It was the eyes. What she had sensed in her soul was undeniable. She had come face to face with evil, and it was real.

Much later in her career she would see that look again in people. But a moment of recognition would come in a flash several years later, while she was walking one evening to a neighboring missionary family's house. On the porch was a huge snake, dead she first thought, probably put there by the teenage son of the family as a prank to scare people.

"All of a sudden this thing starts coming toward me," she says. "And I was just kind of glued to it. And those eyes. It brought to my mind, 'Oh! the same kind of eyes I saw in that man.'"

There was a second realization that stayed with Geneva after her encounter with that man. He thought he had power, but the power really had him. And when the chance of losing him to the one true God appeared, it exercised its claim quickly. The witch doctor with the amazing power suddenly died, mired in his own sins.

Chapter 5

Seeing God's Power

While Geneva was discovering her new field of ministry in Africa, Gordon was discovering the power of spiritual revival back in the U.S. The spiritual events he was a part of during his last year at North Park would become a reference point for the rest of his ministry. Gordon would spend the rest of his life praying for and working for spiritual revival, wherever he was. And he saw it happen. He learned why and when it happens.

Those key lessons began that senior year at North Park.

Gordon and others had been meeting for a year in Anderson Chapel at North Park and praying for revival. During one of those chapel meetings, Gordon recalls, there was an unusual impression felt by everyone attending that God was going to do something.

One week later, which was the week before Thanksgiving vacation in 1949, Gordon and the other members of the summer evangelistic team were to give a report on their summer missions work in Kansas. The meeting started out a disaster. The trio attempted to perform as they had during the summer, but they did an awful job. A duet pairing Gordon and Gordon Johnson was so far off, it was embarrassing. Then Gordon's trumpet performance was bad. The only musical success was a number built around Gordon's whistling, but it sure didn't save the day.

If something moved those people at the meeting, it certainly was not the music! Yet an amazing thing happened.

Gordon stood and gave his brief report on the signs of revivals at other schools in the Northwest. Then he asked those in the audience who wanted revival to go to their knees and ask God for it.

Many of those young people fell to their knees in prayer. "From then on, the meeting was in God's hands," Gordon recalls. "It went on hour after hour, until about 4 a.m., when the last person was prayed for."

The meeting lasted for days, even going into the Thanksgiving break.

Gordon and his friends had to leave that meeting to keep a commitment they had made in the summer. The minister of the Covenant Church in Smolan, Kansas, had asked them to come and help at a week-long revival meeting.

In many churches, annual revival meetings are as predictable as a Christmas Eve service. However, this meeting exploded.

"People poured into the aisles that first night," Gordon recalls. "The spirit fell on the meetings, and they went on for two weeks."

One of the Gordon's fondest memories of that meeting was an encounter he had with a Swedish bachelor farmer. The man came up to Gordon and said they needed to talk, so the two of them stepped over to a corner of the church.

"I thought he wanted to talk to me about some theological issue or something, because one fellow had really taken me to task. He was a Waldenstromian, which was the moral-influence theory of the atonement, and I believe in substitution: Christ died in my place. And that's what I preached.

"But it wasn't a theological issue. He was a farmer, and he had been out in the barnyard, and he said, 'While I was standing out there today, and I was looking at my steers, the Lord showed me one and said, 'Now brother, that one is for Brother Gordon. That one right there.' I said, 'Really?' He said, 'Yes. Now I just have one question. How would you like it? Do you want to take it right now, or do you want me to feed it up, and I'll sell it in the spring and send you a check?'"

Gordon laughs when he recalls the story. "I said, 'Well, I have no way of taking it right now, so would you feed it up, sell it in the spring, and send me the check?'"

Gordon found that year to be a sort of crash course in revival. But in addition to that, he had to decide about his field of missions work. And he could not forget about Geneva.

"I had not the slightest idea how this all was going to work out," Gordon says. "But there was one extenuating factor in all this: China was closing down in 1949. I had already that spring seen a film called "Congo Calls." It was a film produced by the World Mission Department, filmed by one of the missionaries out there, Harvey Widman. And seeing that film, I had already decided, if China closes down — and they're saying it's going to close down because of the communism — I would love to go to Africa.

"It had nothing to do with whether she was there. ... Here was a needy people. I saw all of the references to idolatry in the film, and people who needed the light of Christ. So my thought was, 'If China closes down, go to Africa.' And when we got back (to North Park) that fall, China had definitely closed."

It certainly would be nice, though, having Geneva on the same continent. In fact, Gordon had decided that he would like her to be even closer. Through the letters over the months, their feelings had grown even deeper. They truly were soul-mates, both determined to serve God first and foremost.

He said that finally, while writing one letter, he felt it was time to propose to her. He gulped, and penned the big question, "I'm just wondering if you'd like to change your name to Christensen."

It was a line written with much care, and prayer. He told God that if this marriage was of Him, Gordon would have to get an affirmative answer the first time. This would be the only time he would ever ask, because if the marriage was of God, Geneva would know. She was in touch with Him as well as Gordon.

The letter went in the mail. The wait of weeks began. Study sessions, classes, prayer, work at the Portage Park Covenant Church, meetings of the Missionary Volunteers all came and went. Then, one day, the letter from Africa arrived.

Gordon put it on his desk and would not open it. His roommate that year was Glen Anderson, who went on to become the dean of the seminary at North Park. He saw the letter sitting on the desk.

"Gordy, have you gotten an answer back from Geneva?" he asked.

"Yeah, it's on my desk."

"What did she say?"

"I don't know. I'm scared to open it."

Anderson stared at him. "Gordy, if you don't open that letter, I'm going to open it."

That finally got Gordon to take action. "No you won't! I'm going to open it," he said.

He tore open the envelope and was greeted by the handwriting he had come to love. As he began reading, the words he was hoping for jumped off the page at him: "Yes, I will change my name to Christensen."

He read them again and again. Yes, she would change her name to Christensen. What a great sentence! It was too good to be true, yet there it was, on paper, proof that he wasn't dreaming.

The spring semester was coming to a close. Gordon prepared for work as a missionary in Africa. The Portage Park Covenant Church gathered enough supplies to fill several shipping barrels for Gordon and Geneva on the mission field. Gordon then traveled to New York City, where he had to wait for an Africa-bound ship. From there the ship sailed to New Orleans, where it had a one-week delay waiting for cargo. Then began a three-week voyage that would put him in Matadi about July 18, 1950.

Among the items Gordon carried with him were three beautiful rings he bought in New York City — an engagement ring and the wedding rings for his bride and himself. Gordon and Geneva would have those same rings throughout their careers as missionaries in Africa, and their married lives. Once, on a dark night years later, Gordon would lose his in the sand beside a spring in Africa. A missionary friend would later find it with a flashlight. Over the years, it would also get so bent during different mishaps that Gordon would have to have a friend stretch it back into shape by setting it on a workbench and pounding nail after nail into its circle until it was round enough to get back on Gordon's finger.

The rings would be constant companions through many adventures, hardships and victories as the young couple wearing them grew into a team, giving most of their lifetimes to each other and service in Christ's name in remote Africa.

To pay for the rings, Gordon used the money the bachelor farmer in Smolan mailed him after selling that cow. Ever since, the rings have been a reminder to the missionary couple that the Lord is always able to provide, even before His people realize they have a need.

Life Lessons

Gordon reflected on this chapter of his life and offers these thoughts that others might find useful:

"The God of the infinite is also the God of the infinitesimal. Portage Park Church provided all the incidentals for Geneva and me, and a bachelor farmer provided the money for rings. Never has the Lord failed to provide just what was needed at the right time. Money, friends, intercessors have all appeared just when needed."

Chapter 6

A Rough Start

Gordon's voyage to Africa took three weeks. He landed in Matadi about July 18, and from there headed by train for Leopoldville, where Geneva was waiting for him.

"I will never forget that trip," Gordon says. "I got on the train, and immediately, big blisters started on my lips. By the time I got to Leopoldville, they were large. I thought, this is a funny mess. I'm gonna kiss her with these?"

Traveling with Gordon was a fellow missionary named Hector McMillan. He kidded Gordon a lot during that journey, and the fellowship helped ease Gordon's mind as he thought about all that lay ahead.

Geneva paced at the station as she waited for the train to arrive. Everyone at the Mission House was excited about her meeting Gordon again; their romance had become quite a point of interest at the Mission House and the field station where she was working.

Geneva had kept her engagement a secret because she was one of the only two nurses at the mission station. It had recently lost two others — when they married. Thus Dr. Wally, the station's physician, was prone to grumble about nurses: "They come out and get married, and I lose my nurses." That kept Geneva from sharing the big joy in her life with anyone on the field.

But in December, at an annual conference, a letter arrived saying Gordon Christensen would probably be joining them, and the news was out. Yet Geneva was determined to stay on the field and assist at the hospital, although she didn't know how that would work.

The steam train finally pulled to a stop at the Leopoldville station with a hiss of the brakes. As he stepped off the train, Gordon got his first glimpse of Geneva in nearly a year. "I can see her yet," he says.

All the restraint and understatement that seemed to characterize Geneva went out the window. She ran to him and jumped into his arms — and gave him a hug. The warm kisses would wait.

Their years of adventure together in Africa had officially begun.

Some of the challenges they would face for years had begun as well. The mysterious fever blisters that had struck Gordon were only a precursor to the health problems they would endure for years. And at the time of their reunion at the Leopoldville station, Geneva already had been battling for months bouts of exhaustion and diarrhea. Though she never seemed to shake the illness that first year on the field, she continued her full workload at the hospital.

But this day was one of celebration. Geneva was staying at the Mission House, while Gordon moved into the home of Bert and Jean Ogren, missionaries who would later start the first Protestant publishing house in the Belgian Congo.

"The Ogrens advised us to stay in Leo instead of going to Uganda — then British — where it was necessary to just post marriage 'bans' for two weeks," Gordon says. "If nobody contested the posting, one could get married."

For the rest of July and most of August, Gordon and Geneva made daily trips to the offices of the Belgian government trying to get permission to marry. They had their birth certificates, then had to send for duplicates and then more duplicates. They were sent from one bureau to the next. Finally, a missionary named LeOla Johnson, on her way home at the end of her term, stopped at the Mission House. Her French, as opposed to Gordon's and Geneva's one year in college, was excellent. She agreed to help them and went to the official who would actually be in charge of marrying them — the mayor.

Not even explanations in good French were enough to satisfy this bureaucrat. He wanted documentation from the U.S. government in Washington, D.C., that neither Gordon nor Geneva had been married before!

They told the mayor that there were no such documents available in America, and they would never get such a letter from a Washington official. They did manage to get some letters from county officials back in Kansas saying things like, "To the best of my knowledge ..." but the mayor was not impressed. He wanted it U.S.-government certified that this was Gordon and Geneva's first marriage.

Finally Gordon went to the acting governor of the Belgian Congo and explained his problem. The governor then called the mayor and ordered him to the marry the couple, and the governor would be responsible for any consequences.

The mayor set the date for the ceremony: Sept. 1, 1950, at the Belgian government building, the Hotel DeVille. The mayor arrived in full dress, a white uniform with gold braid, and with all due pomp and ceremony, performed the wedding ceremony.

The entire affair was in French, which Gordon could barely understand. The mayor would say something, and when he looked up, Gordon would say, "Oui!" He had no idea what the mayor was saying or what he was agreeing to.

The mayor knew this and even teased him. "You speak French pretty well, don't you?" he said.

"No!" Gordon admitted, to a great deal of laughter from the guests.

But when it was finished, Gordon and Geneva had a signed wedding contract. Now that the legalities were covered, they could have the church ceremony that meant the most to them.

They went home, baked and decorated a cake, and the next day, Saturday, Sept. 2, 1950 had a church ceremony at the British Baptist Chapel.

The floor was so rough and full of splinters that Geneva bought a bolt of unbleached muslin to roll out as a rug for her. The church was decorated with gladiolas and carnations that the local florist's shop had gotten from Belgium. She had a bouquet, and Gordon wore a boutonniere given to him by one of the missionaries. It was so big that Geneva says it could have passed for a corsage. And the well-scrubbed church, which had been home to a bunch of bats until only the the day before, sparkled in the glow of a candelabra and the African afternoon sun.

Having challenged the government authorities already, now it was time to challenge the social order. In those days,

Gordon and Geneva on the day of their church wedding, September 2, 1950.

Africans were never involved in such ceremonies. The Belgian authorities and white settlers clearly saw the Africans as inferiors, and they let it be known through segregation and displays of contempt.

"It was pathetic," Geneva says. "There was the old-school mentality of the Belgian government. 'The African is over there, and I sit over here at my nice table.' We said, 'That's not what we've come here for; they're going to be in our wedding party.' A lot of people kind of looked askance at it. Africans were in our wedding party, they were our ushers ... the director of the Mission House then was African, and that couple came as guests, with several others."

Not fully realizing it, Gordon and Geneva had taken head-on what had been one of the biggest obstacles to moving the Gospel in the Belgian Congo — racism. The Africans resented the contempt they saw in the eyes of many of the white people in their land. But here were some white people who were different; they were ambassadors for Christ.

After the ceremony, at which the Ogrens served as best man and bridesmaid, the Ogrens also hosted a reception at their home.

It had been an exhausting time of government rigmarole, decorating the church and helping with the reception. After the Saturday wedding, they stayed in Leopoldville and went shopping Monday for the missionaries on the field. Once those supplies were loaded onto a boat, they flew the 900 miles from Leopoldville to Libenge and then started a truck ride for Karawa and the mission station.

It was a harrowing ride for Gordon. The truck roared down a one-lane, winding path through an African plain that was thick with elephant grass about 10 feet high. All vision was obscured by the tall grass on a ride that felt like a combination of a maze, an airboat ride through the Everglades or a hightailing race through a hundred-square-mile cornfield in Iowa. Gordon was seeing how really far from civilization they would be.

They traveled through Bau, then Bokada and finally arrived in Karawa.

The houses at the Karawa mission station were made of whitewashed mud with grass roofs, so the station looked like a village of little cottages. Abundant flowers were planted around them and lined dirt pathways. One structural exception was the Thornbloom family's home, which was built of burned brick.

The huts at Karawa were arranged in a rectangle, and the missionaries called the grassy center of the village Times Square. The African population was about 500, and there were about 15 missionaries and their children.

Karawa was the hub of the Ngbaka tribe, most of which believed in animism; they thought there were spirits everywhere and for everything. There was a spirit of the waterfall, a spirit of hunting, and so forth.

"When we drove into Karawa, we were greeted by Elmer Pearson on his motorcycle, a Harley Davidson," Gordon says. "And he led the motorcade, which was him and us, up into Karawa to a rousing reception by what must have been hundreds of Africans and missionaries. That was my introduction to missionary work out there in Karawa."

Elmer Pearson became a close friend and mentor to Gordon. Elmer was about 30, and Gordon had just turned 25 when he arrived on the field. Elmer was a member of the Covenant Church and was from California.

"He was an optimist, an excellent mentor," Gordon says. "He can pick you up and tell you, 'You're doing great, just keep going.'"

Elmer also had a great sense of fun. He loved roaring through the jungle on his Harley, and he was full of jokes. "Sometimes he would ride by a village and yell, 'Vote for Snodgrass!' and the people would smile and wave," Gordon says. "Then he would turn and say to me, 'See, I've got them!'"

Geneva's year of service before Gordon's arrival proved a great blessing to him. Geneva was able to teach him much of the trade language — Lingala — during their six weeks in Leopoldville. He continued to practice his Lingala with Geneva and an African translator for another two weeks in Karawa.

Then Elmer told him, "It's time for you to preach."

"They didn't let you wait around in those days," Gordon recalls with laughter. "I said, 'Preach?' and he said, 'Yeah. You just write it out, and then I'll take you out on the motorcycle and some evening you can get up and preach.' So I wrote out a one- or two-page message in Lingala. I had Geneva look it over, and the African informant. We went out on his Harley, and we had an evening service."

The village Gordon visited was about 20 minutes from Karawa on a rutted, red dirt road. About 100 or 120 people had packed the meeting house, which was a rectangular, adobe mud building about 40 feet by 20 feet with a grass roof. Its raised platform was made of hardened mud.

The congregation sang songs, and then Elmer got up and introduced Gordon in their tribal language, Ngbaka (pronounced BAH-ka). As Gordon read his sermon in Lingala, either Elmer or a native pastor translated it on into Nbgaka.

That first message was on salvation: God sent his son to die on the cross, and our work was to accept what he had done, and we would be new people.

That was the beginning. But challenges to Gordon's and Geneva's health were beginning as well.

Within a month of his arrival, Gordon contracted hepatitis. Geneva continued working in the hospital and taking care of him at home. Her own illness continued to worsen until three months after their marriage, she was bedridden with a disease that at that time was difficult to diagnose — amoebic dysentery. She had apparently contracted it in Libenge while caring for one of her first patients, missionary Sandy Widman, who had cerebral malaria. Geneva had eaten raw vegetables in a salad at a restaurant in that African city, unaware that missionaries were advised to never eat anything that was not cooked.

The dysentery supposedly had returned with soldiers who had fought in North Africa during World War II. It was transmitted by food, flies and impure water. Soap was still rare after the war, and hands were often unwashed, even among restaurant workers.

She carried the disease for nine months until she could no longer get up. By this time, she was extremely sick and pregnant as well. Dr. Wally, the clinic doctor, thought she might die.

Geneva remembers waking up one night and finding Gordon sitting at her bedside, weeping. She told him she was going to be all right and encouraged him to get on with his missionary work in the villages.

Geneva remembers taking Gordon's anguish personally, thinking she had to get up and going so he wouldn't feel so badly. But there was no way.

"I was really stupid in many respects," Geneva says. "Because he felt so badly, I'd tell him, 'Go out on that village trip. I'll be fine here by myself.' I didn't want to hinder his progress in the missionary work. In the daytime, there was an African who would be around the house. But not at night."

Gordon was sick himself and very demoralized. He continued making his preaching trips to jungle villages, usually accompanied by an African, but it seemed whenever he left, a disaster struck at home, where Geneva lay bedridden and alone.

The worst disaster was an attack of driver ants.

Driver ants lived in giant ant hills, and when they were on the move, they could be seen traveling in single or double file. But they would swarm when they converged on a house or chicken coop in their search for food. One night while Gordon was away and Geneva was home alone, the ants swarmed on the house.

"It was terrible," Geneva says. "I was so weak, and I was absolutely covered in driver ants. I got on an Army field telephone that was almost worse than nothing — you had to pour water on the wires to get it to work!"

The night watchman and June Pearson, who apparently had heard Geneva's S.O.S. on the telephone, came to help, holding her up on her feet while brushing the ants off her. June took Geneva to spend the night with her family. To get the ants away from the Christensen house, the missionaries poured a narrow trail of kerosene around the outside.

From that night on, nurse Gerda Wahrgren stayed with Geneva whenever Gordon was away. She never asked; she would just show up and sleep on the davenport.

Gerda had just returned for her second term after having studied tropical medicine in Antwerp, Belgium. The medical community was just learning about amoebic dysentery; it had not even known what the jungle disease looked like under the microscope. But Gerda had learned of a possible treatment for it; shots of a powerful drug called Emetine. In Geneva's case, an early term pregnancy, they had no clue of what the impact would be on the baby.

Gerda gave Geneva the shots three times a day, leaving painful, dark lumps. Geneva also received enemas in an effort to heal her damaged digestive tract.

Geneva kept her word to Gordon: she got better as promised. The shots healed the dysentery. All she needed now was recuperation time.

This she had as she spent most of her time in bed or on a cot.

It was also a time of refocusing for Geneva. She had known all along that marriage was going to alter her ministry, but she didn't know how. She had been deeply concerned about marriage being a hindrance to her work as a mission nurse. But she did have one comfort: she was confident her decision to marry Gordon was right in God's sight.

She had prayed that God would have to bring Gordon to Africa if she was to marry him, and that he was in Africa because the other door of ministry, China, had closed. She wanted him to be in Africa because he was called to serve there, not because she was there. In a sense, she had put a fleece before the Lord regarding Gordon, a practice she doesn't promote and that she now thinks indicates her spiritual immaturity at age 24. But God was gracious, and He worked with her where she was. The door to China had closed; Gordon had a heart and vision for bringing the Gospel to Africa. It gave her great confidence to step into marriage and eliminated any doubts that she had been called to be a missionary and that marrying Gordon was right.

She was now convinced that these foundational facts were beyond dispute. God had verified them for her in a very personal way. She was confident she was in harmony with God's plan.

In her head, she knew these things. Now there was time for them to sink into her heart. She was changing position, but that didn't mean she was being benched while Gordon carried the ball.

Yet Geneva had to conquer feelings of frustration. In a sense she felt like a failure because she was not able to help Gerda Wahrgren at the hospital. She was the only nurse on duty while Geneva was sick, and guilt gnawed at Geneva incessantly while she was bedridden. In addition to feeling she should be at work at the hospital, Geneva also felt she had become a harmful distraction to Gordon as he tried to establish contact with villages in that area.

Geneva also came to realize that much of what was haunting her was her own pride. She had planned to be the young woman who proved that a missionary could be happily married and effective on the mission field. She was going to be a missionary nurse, selflessly caring for the sick morning, noon and night in the name of Jesus Christ. This had been her focus since age 12. Now that focus was changing and doors were closing, sometimes in very harsh ways:

She was literally yanked out of the hospital routine by illness. Geneva does not believe God sends amoebic dysentery. But she does believe that her drive to be working in the hospital was so strong, that if God were calling her to another role, she could well have ignored it in her dogged determination to fulfill a self-set role. Instead, she was flat on her back for weeks, "of no use to anyone," she says, and then a month recuperating afterward.

She was going to be a young mother in Africa. Images flashed before her of the people who had said those young wives and mothers on the mission field didn't really "do the work." She remembered the sad young woman she had met in nurses' training whose parents were missionaries to China, and how they had sent her to the U.S. to live in boarding schools so they could "do the work," and how that longtime separation had left the girl scared to meet her mother and father. Would Geneva be able to provide in a foreign, dangerous land the kind loving family she had known?

These were deep struggles. The weeks of recuperation, like the six weeks in Leopoldville awaiting state permission to marry, were a time of thinking, talking, planning and prayer — a time of spiritual reorganization that helped hone the young couple into a sharper tool.

Early in the new year, Geneva started joining Gordon on his village visits. She would use the time while Gordon was talking to the people to do hospital bookwork, a cumbersome task required by the Belgian bureaucracy. She would set up a dispensary and treat people for common maladies such as diaharrea, scabies, ringworm, intestinal parasites, malaria, and a very ugly body ulcer called yaws, caused by a spirochete that could get into the skin and eat away at it very rapidly.

Her trips to the villages also let Geneva start to see the lives of the women and children in Africa. She could observe quietly while her husband talked about the Gospel to the men of the village. The women would often run and hide at the sight of strangers, or giggle and watch from behind a hut or tree. Yet as Geneva stayed, meeting with them and their children, she began to understand African women, to see the low worth placed upon them and children by African culture. And she recognized that Jesus deeply wanted to reach these overlooked people, even though it would be in opposition to a society that oppressed them.

Life Lessons

One of the essentials Gordon and Geneva carried with them into Africa was a lack of doubt.

Geneva says she never doubted her calling or questioned God that she was where she was supposed to be. "That is why I tell young people, 'Be sure that God has called you, because there will be strenuous times, and testing will come. If you start doubting your calling then, it could be your undoing.

"I had great confidence regarding my calling and my marriage. I believe this was built up through the Word and prayer."

One of the essentials they had to learn on the mission field was to be submissive to God's will. This was easier said than done, because Gordon and Geneva had shown up with such noble goals. Yet even the noble goals we may select for ourselves may not be attainable by the course we set ourselves. They may not even be directions God wants us to go.

Believers do have some promises from God, however, that if we submit ourselves to His plan, we won't be disappointed or forced into a service that we detest.

> *Commit thy way unto the Lord; trust also in him; and he shall bring it to pass. And he shall bring forth thy righteousness as the light, and thy judgment as the noonday.*
> — Psalm 37:5-6

> *Fear thou not; for I am with thee: be not dismayed; for I am thy God: I will strengthen thee; yea, I will help thee; yea, I will uphold thee with the right hand of my righteousness ... For I the Lord thy God will hold thy right hand, saying unto thee, Fear not; I will help thee.* — Isaiah 41:10, 13

> *Ye have not chosen me, but I have chosen you, and ordained you, that ye should go and bring forth fruit, and that your fruit should remain: that whatsoever ye shall ask of the Father in my name, he may give it you.* — John 15:16

Thus, God makes it possible for us to enter into a state of "confident submissiveness," a contradiction in the world's eyes.

But it also means we shouldn't be fooled by the nobility of our self-set goals. We can make even entering the ministry a career of self-set goals and source of self pride. In Geneva's case, it was hospital work on the mission field.

"Far too much of my focus, for too long, had been on 'the work.' All through my training years, and the mission field, which had been training years, the Lord has had to show me what 'the work' is. He was trying to call me to be submissive to Himself so he could get a message through."

Geneva says that in hindsight, she can even see how that time of sickness became something of value in the hands of God. She said that while she was sick, she often thought of a verse in Psalm 119:

> "It is good for me that I have been afflicted, that I might learn thy law."

In hindsight, she sees that God can make even a satanic attack into fertile ground for growth. His creative and redemptive power is limitless.

Letters Home

This is a letter, dated Dec. 18, 1950, from Gordon to Rev. Ralph P. Hanson at Covenant headquarters in Chicago, along with a traveling expense report that totaled $377.26:

Dear Rev. Hanson;

Here it is, nigh six months since I left American soil, and it does seem a long time.

There are many discouraging things about the work out here – viz., the prevalence of sin among the church members, – and leaders, the inability of so many of the church members to read the Word of God, the opposition, etc., but there are many encouraging signs, which counterbalance the discouragements, so we 'thank God, and take courage.'

I have been out in the villages for Big Sundays, one village trip, and Norm Barram and I are going out this week again for another village trip, to different places, respectively. We are planning our schedule so that one couple of the evangelism couples are out in the villages all the time, that is, at least one of the couples is out on a preaching and teaching mission at all times. So far, that has worked acceptably.

Attached is a statement of expenses which I incurred enroute to Congo. I have forgotten whether or not I was reimbursed for the passport photos and payment to the Belgian Consulate or not. Also, the statement of expenses to Leopoldville is merely for the time from arrival until the earliest possible departure by boat, and is not for the entire time I was in Leo getting attached.

Greetings to all at Covenant Headquarters at this Christmas season, – we are receiving most welcome packages from home, and thanks for the greetings from Headquarters.

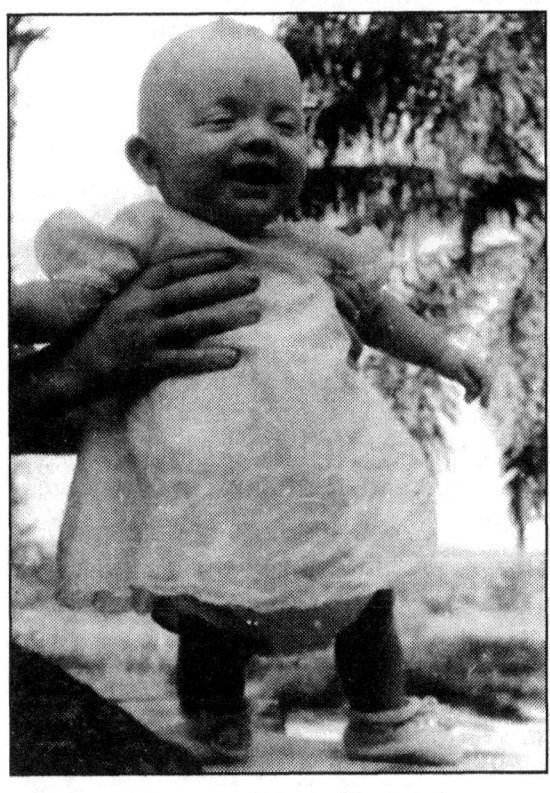

Susan Christensen, 1951.

CHAPTER 7

A REVIVAL IN THE LAND

Susan Christensen was born in perfect health May 29, 1951. Geneva delivered her at the Karawa mission hospital with the help of Dr. Wally and nurse Gerda Wahrgren. Susan was destined to have a life different than most; she would grow up a white child immersed in the African culture of the

Congo bush. Her parents, as missionaries, had decided before her birth that if the Lord did bless them with children, they were going to be a part of the missionary team — no staying home while the parents went away.

But it wasn't long before Susan started to meet her relatives as well. Geneva's sister, Evelyn, arrived in Bangui May 26, 1951, to start work as the Covenant Church's first missionary called specifically to serve as a teacher for missionary children. It took several days for her to reach the mission station, and she arrived the morning after Susan's birth.

The family had heard how sick Geneva was, and they were concerned about her health and the baby. Geneva had not offered a due date because she did not know what effect her sickness would have on Susan, and Geneva thought a due date could just cause her parents more worry.

When Evelyn arrived at the mission station, everyone but Geneva was there to greet her. Evelyn nearly panicked. She thought something had happened and she had not been told. Gordon assured her Geneva was all right, put her on a Cushman motor scooter and took her to the house.

Evelyn rushed into the house and was so excited to see her sister alive that she didn't even notice the baby in the basket beside the bed and almost knocked it over. It was a happy, memorable reunion — and introduction.

Evelyn lived with Gordon and Geneva in a spare room at the house. She had a delightful time with Susan. One of the things that had made leaving home hard for Evelyn was saying goodbye to a newborn niece that she loved.

At age 3 months, Susan Christensen may have become history's youngest missionary. That was her age when she made her first trip with Gordon and Geneva to an African village.

"It was great," Geneva says. "Most of the Africans had never seen a white baby."

Other missionaries thought the Christensens were taking too many risks by carrying Susan into the bush with them. But this was how they had chosen to live and do God's work. There were no ways to avoid risk in life, particularly life in Africa.

> *The fear of man bringeth a snare: but whoso putteth his trust in the Lord shall be safe.* — Proverbs 29:25

It is on such Biblical promises that Gordon and Geneva based their decisions. And it didn't take long for them to see what a huge difference Susan made in their effectiveness.

She drew the Africans to her, bringing down barriers between the villagers and missionaries. Through this mutual love for children and fascination with new life, a common bond was established.

"Everybody had to hold her," Geneva says. "I put her in some pretty unclean hands. But what I learned to do early on was put her in a little receiving blanket, and hand her right down the line. Everyone had a chance to hold her. Then I took her back, and I'd go back in the hut, and I'd take this blanket off and put her in the buggy. I'd put the mosquito net over it, and then I told them, 'Our babies aren't accustomed to being held all the time.' Which was true; we put them down. Now they normally hold a baby all the time, because they don't have anyplace to put them."

But everyone was content to have held the baby once and gotten a close look at this unusual child.

"Afterward, when I would go out, I would have her in the buggy, and they'd get to push. As many little hands as could touch that buggy would be holding onto it. And we would go walking through the village."

Once when Susan was a little older, Gordon and Geneva went to visit the Ngombe (pronounced GOMbeh) Lisala tribe, which had been hostile to missionaries in the past.

"They had threatened one of the men of our tribe who went down there to preach to them. In fact, they were going after him with spears," Geneva says. "He happened to have a little hand-cranked phonograph from the group Gospel Recordings, and he put this record on and started winding it. They put their spears down and started to listen. ... But they were so angry at the Ngbaka tribe, because, they said, 'The missionaries came there first, and your tribe is proliferating, and our tribe is dying out. We haven't had any help for our needs.'

"We were trying to get into this area, but because they were so angry because they had not been given help earlier, they were not very receptive. But having that baby really broke the ice."

Gordon and Geneva were planning to stay for two weeks or so. "At that place, who was going to come hear the Gospel, when basically they were not welcoming us? But when they saw that baby, and got to hold her, and I would take her and put her in the buggy and push to the end of the village, I had so many people when I came back. He would start preaching, and we had a whole congregation. We called it baby buggy evangelism."

Geneva brought a nurse with her on the trip, and they set up a dispensary. "Then I realized we had come right into an epidemic of measles. I thought, 'Oh, this is not what I need with this little baby.'"

It was an unforeseen risk, but Susan did not get the measles. However, the couple had stepped into a foreseeable risk, a hostile village, and did so knowingly.

Geneva says, "I think I had a lot greater faith at that time than I had at other times, you know. Because I was absolutely convinced that where God opened the door for us to go, He would protect us. And we went. Some missionaries did have a problem with that kind of attitude, and they thought we were being foolhardy."

"But there was another thing true," Gordon says. "There was a lot more prayer going on in those days among the missionary body than even today. The first Tuesday of every month was a whole day of prayer. We stopped everything and spent the whole day in prayer. And that made a tremendous impact."

"That included the Africans wherever you were located," Geneva says. "We made up a program so that every hour there was a different leader down at the church, or a missionary, or at home in small groups, and we had specific things that we were praying for, and we saw God work. And I think, in those days, too, we expected hardship.

"When I left my home that day of my brother's wedding, my pastor said, 'Now let's pray for you today before you leave that you will not get sick out there.' My first thought was, 'Now wouldn't that be great?'

"I said, 'No, I don't think that would be a wise prayer. If I would not get sick, how would I relate to them when they are sick?' ... So we didn't pray, but before that term was over, I began to wonder if I'd made a mistake!"

Nevertheless, she thinks that the Africans learned by seeing the Lord working in missionaries' lives whether in sickness or health. In fact, the proof of their human frailty was vital to the moving of the Gospel in Africa.

Geneva says this became clear at the centennial anniversary of missionary work in the Belgian Congo by the Swedish Covenant.

In the early days of the work, the mortality rate among missionaries was so high that the Swedes would build their own wooden coffins before they left for the field, using them as steamer trunks during the trip. The mortality rate among those early missionaries was 50 percent within two years. But at that anniversary celebration, the missionaries learned that the death rate was due not only to malaria, diarrhea, tuberculosis or sleeping sickness.

"This one old man stood up and said, 'I need to make known to you what we did, because there have been questions about why so many Swedish missionaries died,'" Geneva recalls. "'When they came, these white people, we had to find out if they were real. If they were real, like us, and came with this kind of message, then we could listen. The only way to find out if they were real and not some spirit was to poison them like we poisoned one another. If they died, they were real.'"

With each death, a missionary's message was silenced — but not for long. More missionaries would come, bringing their own coffins and the message of the Gospel. The Africans finally were convinced they were real and had a message that they valued more than their own lives.

Geneva says, "In those early days, there had to be a commitment that we seldom deal with today."

While the first missionaries showed they were prepared to die to share the Gospel, future generations would have to show by daily example how to live by it.

Prayer. Commitment. Confidence in God's calling. All these things were part of daily living with the African people. They were ingredients in decisions and discussions large and small. And they caused some big things to happen in the Belgian Congo in the early 1950s.

In 1951 a revival swept the Congo region where the Covenant Church was working: villages and mission stations such as Gbado, Businga, Karawa and Gbado. It began, Gordon says, as all great revivals begin. A few people humbled themselves and began to pray. One of the missionaries at the Bau station, which was a Free Church station, and an African pastor named Mobaya, began committing much of their time to daily prayer.

It was a time of deep concern for the church at Karawa. It was the oldest mission station, and, Geneva says, had become probably the most hardened.

"Just a tremendous carnal nature was coming up in the church," she says. "They had been Christians now for a while, some of them maybe 20 years, and they had kind of gotten over the excitement that they could be delivered from all of the evils and darkness they had come out of. Some of them were starting to get lax in their faith and wanted to revert back and pick up bits and pieces of their old culture and nature that they liked, that satisfied the flesh. We were having a real problem."

During this time of prayer, the missionary and Pastor Mobaya were fasting through breakfast and lunch, eating only dinner.

The missionary began to get criticism from the others on the mission station for not being more involved. Geneva recalls the missionaries discussing how they all would like to spend their time in prayer, but there were problems to resolve.

"I think some of us were wondering, 'What is going on?' He was so intent on this revival goal. And, of course, those of us who had not been in that intensive prayer and Bible study, we didn't understand it.

"They hadn't seen the benefit of it yet," Geneva says.

It wasn't long before they did, however. In 1951, the pastors from the Free Church, which worked in Africa alongside the Covenant missionaries, had a retreat at the Kala mission station for a time of refreshment in prayer, Bible study, confession and restoration. Covenant pastors, including Pastor Mobaya and his missionary prayer partner, also attended.

"When we gathered at Kala mission station, the Lord sent a spirit of revival to all of these preachers. In fact, they were weeping uncontrollably and confessing sin, and coldness, and lethargy and all the rest. Well, that was the beginning of revival, and from that point on, revival spread to Gbado, Bau and other Free Church stations."

The men from Karawa and Gbado also met once at Kwada, the clear-water lake, for days of intense prayer and semi-fasting, then again at the Gbado mission station. Geneva and the women who stayed at Karawa also dedicated their time to prayer.

"I remember we were all in one place praying, and said, 'Can the Lord do anything for Karawa?' And about that time we heard He had really spoken up there at Gbado and revival had started there."

It was at Gbado that the revival broke out on the Covenant field. In the midst of the men's meeting, missionary schoolteacher Vanette Thorsell came in and announced that a revival had begun — among a group of secular high school students. There had been no pastor there leading them as this began in their classrooms, but there was a movement of the Spirit among them, a softening of hearts, confession of sins.

That night the men returned to Karawa.

"The next morning normally we had chapel at 5:30, so Gordon had gone down to chapel," Geneva says. She had stayed home with Susan, but was outside on her way to the cookhouse when she heard a startling noise. "It was like a waterfall going by you: crescendos, and up and down. And I thought, 'What in the world am I hearing?' I looked around, and there was no seeming wind. I didn't see any big fires burning, because that can sometimes create a wind pattern. Then it dawned on me. I thought, 'Hey, a revival's coming!'

"I don't know why I equated that with revival, but I remember getting the baby and sticking her in the buggy and grabbing a bottle or two of milk because I thought I might be there awhile, and I took off because we lived a ways from the church.

"I went pushing that buggy down to the church, and I could not believe my eyes ... there were people packed all outside. Now there had not even been any notice of any meeting; we didn't expect a meeting. It was going to be a normal morning chapel with a handful of workers.

"The closer I got to the church, the more I heard this sound. It was just going in waves, and I realized it was almost like a wailing of the people. It was different, totally different from the death wail we were very familiar with.

"I thought, 'How can I even get close to that church?' It was so thick with people. When I came with the baby buggy, they were very gracious and made a path for me, which I shouldn't have had any more privilege getting up close than they did, but I got up to the church, and I was dumfounded. People were packed like sardines, and there was no preaching going on as I recall it. It was loud — they would weep, sort of, then it would crescendo and then it would die down. Then it would begin again, like a mourning situation, but a little different, too.

"I do remember Pastor Mobaya stood up and read a few verses, but that was about the extent of it. And this went on and on and on."

The entire event was occurring about dawn, but some of the people at the chapel apparently had started walking at 3 a.m. to arrive there by 5:30. Geneva says that afterward she and others started asking from where these people had come. The villagers had come from miles.

"We asked, 'How come you're at church at Karawa at this hour of the morning?' They said, 'We can't explain it. It was just as though we were being drawn to come here.' There was no human explanation: they had come from miles around. They had walked in darkness."

Geneva says the episode made her think of a passage in the Gospel of John:

> *No man can come to me, except the Father which hath sent me draw him: and I will raise him up at the last day.* — John 6:44

A similar event had occurred at Gbado, and some of the group that had come to Karawa that night were from Gbado. But there was no meeting called; such communication was impossible. Nor did the people have any idea what had happened at Gbado or any other stations.

"God was doing a work, a lot of work, and it was drawing whole families," Geneva says. "There was a lot of revelation about family togetherness during that revival that opened their eyes to a lot. ... People were even weeping, and there are very few tears seen in Africa, even at times of repentance from sin.

"We had no idea what was in the hearts of these people, because we did not know these people that well at that time. Certainly we didn't understand what was going on a lot."

The most apparent work being done was revitalizing and redirecting family relationships. It was as if setting solid family foundations was the next phase of God's agenda for these Africans, and the missionaries happened to be in the audience the day God revealed His hand at work.

One episode that Geneva recalls involved a man named Kongawi.

"I recall him sitting on that bench at the church," she says. "He had been sitting there I don't know how long. Finally, he asked someone if they would go out to the village and bring his wife in, because he had sent her back (to her own family, in effect, divorcing her) because the relationship was so bad. And he said, 'I will not move off of this bench until you go get her and bring her here so I can ask her forgiveness.' And that was the kind of thing that was going on there. It was really astounding."

The mission station virtually shut down as this revival meeting stretched on for days. "This went on for a week, I guess," Geneva says. "Eating wasn't even important. If people had to leave a while, they were back to that church."

Later that first day, Geneva had to take Susan home and go check on the hospital. Everything at the station was running at bare minimum.

"We had an African helper (at the house), and I don't know if he even came that day. But when he did come, he apologized profoundly. He said, 'I haven't even come to the house, but I have been so busy. I have been counseling and praying with people night and day.' He was a deacon. "I said, 'That is wonderful. Keep on as long as the spirit of God is moving.' So everything for those days was just an intense focus on God. A lot of cleaning up."

The results reached far into the bush. Some of the native pastors who were at Karawa when revival broke out there would take off and travel for weeks, seeking out distant relatives or others. Once they had overcome obstacles in their own lives, they would set off on personal missions to spread the Gospel. A lot of the future leadership of the church became established at this time.

The revival went on in some places for a year and a half to two years, Gordon says, although the most intense time was in the beginning, and it did not continue at the explosive level with which it began. In fact, an explosion might be the best way to envision what happened spiritually. After the initial white-hot blast, the repercussions rippled across the Congo and could be felt for about two years.

To Gordon, the Congo revival of 1951 felt like something he had been prepared for throughout his life. He had seen the revival at North Park while he was in college: how it looked, felt and sounded; how it changed people, seeming to give them a new freedom and empowerment, as if they had been healed and strengthened in their souls; how the presence of God seemed as evident as the presence of a strong wind that bends the trees it touches.

"I am the product of revival," Gordon says. "The people who were my mentors were immediate products of revival. Some people have said their early experience in church has almost been a disaster, but for me, I can count person after person after person in the Covenant churches who were revival products and praying people. For example, in the First

Covenant Church in Seattle, the president of the lumber company was the chairman of the church. He was the product of revival. The president of the Moline Elevator Co. of the North Pacific area, he was the product of revival. I'll never forget him. Stately gentleman, who when he would pray or talk, he would weep and cry out to God. That was impressive. These were people way up the ladder socially, economically, and yet they had a bold witness for Christ."

Gordon also had seen touches of revival throughout his life. "Not only the revival at North Park, but there were revivals at camps. Among high school camps. We had seen touches of revival before. And I think all of this was preparation for revival ministry, which is where I think we are at this present time."

LIFE LESSONS

Gordon sees us entering a time of darkness like Africa has left, a time of moral darkness brought on by trust in wealth. He is hoping for a new revival that will even reach into the moral and political realm.

> *If my people, which are called by my name, shall humble themselves, and pray, and seek my face, and turn from their wicked ways; then will I hear from heaven, and will forgive their sin, and will heal their land.* — 2 Chronicles 7:14

It took a supernatural touch of God to inspire, revitalize, and reorient the Congolese people in the 1950s. Missionaries had come and spent their lives in Africa with the people, and yet after half a century, even the Christians were reverting to the pagan ways that had brought such misery before.

This is not unique to the African people — it is common of all people. Ever since the first man, Adam, mankind has had a tradition of turning away from God. The Bible is full of the accounts, and Gordon and Geneva, who have had a perspective on two disparate cultures of the late 20th century, have noticed the United States turning away as so many have before. Yet, as God gave them reason to hope while they were in Africa in the 1950s, they also see reasons to be hopeful for America in the 2000s and beyond.

One of the "wicked ways" from which Africa had to turn — and needed God's help to do so — was in personal relationships. All relationships, including family relationships, were based not on love, but need. If a person was not useful, he or she was not wanted, and if not wanted, then abandoned. Crude forms of abortion and euthanasia were a part of African life. Marriage was based on the need to have children — which were useful as laborers early in life and as a Social Security provider later on. Young women were valuable to a family, who sold them off as wives for prices that a young man might spend the rest of his life paying. He got a mother for children, a homemaker, and free labor. If a man missed payments to his wife's family, the family commonly sent for the woman on some pretext, such as a family member was dying, and then held her until the marriage payments were caught up.

The rapport between husband and wife was not based on love, so marriages were often bitter and strained. Children who were not born perfect were abandoned to die. Since women were married for their usefulness, "unuseful" women were sent back to their families or kicked out. Likewise, polygamy was common among men with money.

The view of human life as a resource even made cannibalism rational — and common. Gordon and Geneva routinely encountered people whose teeth had been sharpened to fang-like points in childhood for eating human meat.

"The killing and eating of others was being done in secret, although the government fought it and made it illegal," Geneva says. "There were jailings and whippings as a result. But people were a food supply."

Gordon says anthropologists would say that cannibalism was really just sacramental, that cannibals would eat a portion of a slain enemy, like the liver, to get his strength. But an ex-cannibal Gordon talked to said that explanation is hogwash.

Gordon recalls the man telling him, "We ate them because we liked them. They were good chop (food)."

"Anthropologists may come and spend two weeks, or even a year, but they don't have the half-century perspective," Gordon says. "He doesn't see them going from eating each other as a sport to loving one another in the church."

Gordon and Geneva take exception to behavioral scientists who come to the defense of cultures such as the one they found in Africa. The Christensens have no dispute with traditions of dress or music, art or occupation. Their concerns are not about how Africans' homes look or church services sound. Their break with the defenders of foreign cultures comes when they see the cultural traditions shackling and destroying people. The Congolese people Gordon and Geneva found in the 1950s were enslaved by a culture that viewed life as a cheap commodity, a tool to be used for survival. In their view, defending such values is like defending slavery.

As a result of simply applying their biblical beliefs faithfully, as they had been taught from childhood, Gordon and Geneva actually were champions in the late '40s and early '50s of such "American" causes as civil rights and the condemnation of racial prejudice, which didn't grab the American psyche until the late '50s and early '60s; of women's rights, which came to the fore in the '60s and '70s; of children's rights, surfacing as a top issue on the West's cultural agenda in the '80s and '90s. As cast today by social planners, stripped of spiritual foundations, those issues can often seem at odds with Judeo-Christian teaching. Not so. Instead, they are —

or were supposed to be — a part of the Christian heritage since the days when Jesus modeled a respect and value for women and children that contradicted the culture of his day. When God is cut out of the equation, these Godly values start to warp into political movements that can become a wedge, splitting families, substituting utilitarianism in relationships for a bond of love — in short, driving a culture more in the direction of old Africa.

Gordon and Geneva have often marvelled during short stints back to the U.S. at the growing similarities they saw between the old African culture and what U.S. culture was becoming. The first innocent surprise was the similarities they noted between pop songs and the African music. Then they started to note strains in relationships, belligerence of young people toward parents and adults (something they had encountered in Africa). Then pagan beliefs getting a foothold in the U.S., a turning to spiritism, a cheapening of human life.

Their brief trips home after years in Africa would provide them something like snapshots or slides of American life clicking by them in a slide show. The deterioration of the culture was easy to see when you weren't immersed in it.

In the late 1990s, however, they see a revival coming. There is a swelling urge to pray. Prayer was coming out of the closet.

Evidence: Frank Perretti's novel *This Present Darkness* showed the power of prayer, and its commercial success stunned the publishing industry when it was released in the 1980s. Its impact was so profound that it turned around the industry regarding Christian fiction.

"Concerts of prayer" are filling stadiums in cities as people come to the mass prayer services. On a personal level, Gordon and Geneva, together with about 30 other associates, have been working through the Department of Prayer and Evangelism of the Covenant Church to present seminars on prayer at churches across the nation. Twenty five years ago, prayer was not an integral part of ministry at many churches. In America, that is reversing in the 1990s.

How do Gordon and Geneva envision American culture changing if the revival they expect comes to pass?

"Well, if the church is prepared to disciple the thousands of converts that will be coming in, then the first change will be a belief in moral absolutes," says Gordon. "Right will be right and wrong will be wrong. And it will be determined by the Word of God."

Gordon says he thinks that step will lead to a society with more compassion. As an example he cited a dispute under way in Wheaton, Ill., where a halfway house has been opened, much to the concern of the neighborhood. A Bible study is being held at the halfway house, and opponents are calling the Bible study a form of counseling. That would make the halfway house a counseling center, which has been declared an inappropriate use of the property.

"In a revival, there will be so many solidly converted that their compassion will reach out to these people instead of rejecting them," Gordon says.

But to erase hardheartedness toward others would first require a supernatural removal of its cause: fear.

"We are getting to be a prison within our own society because there is so much crime," Geneva points out. "I think everyone has this mentality, that if we allow anything of this kind (like the halfway house), it will jeopardize our security. I can understand this for families."

"The problem in our society is we don't have any protection," Gordon says. "There is a spiritual protection a Christian family has, and the ungodly family does not have it. They are well aware that the only protection they have is the laws of the city and the government.

"We look for a greater protection. People have asked us over and over again, 'Wasn't it dangerous in Africa?' That is like asking, 'Do you have to pay to get on a plane?' The answer is obvious.

"There were snakes all over the place, for example. Not once, to my knowledge, has a missionary of the Covenant Church been bitten by a snake, except a short-termer who tried to grab one by the head for fun. Why is it that we haven't been killed by snakes? We go out in the gardens, out in the jungles."

Gordon has had snakes wrap around his legs or slither between his feet as he walked. "But we've never had anyone killed. We have a protection. Here, people are screaming whenever they think there is a sex offender around. Well, talk about it! What are missionaries going into? They are going into the worst of places to see the best of results."

"And this is what I anticipate coming, that there will be a sense of, Hey, God is with us!'"

Thus a revived America would exhibit more compassion. More freedom. Less fear. Less fear to be compassionate.

The key is having trust in God and living covered by intercessory prayer.

"As missionaries we have had devil-possessed people come up and say they would kill us. We'd say, 'You can't, the blood of Jesus covers us.' And they would stand there helpless, while others could be mangled by them. They'd say, 'We'll tear the clothes off you.' We'd say, 'You can't because these clothes belong to Jesus. Try it! You can't!' And they would get their hands close to the clothes ... Couldn't do it. One grabbed hold of my pants, and had them twisted, and I said, 'You've got to let go.' And to watch his hand unfurl and back off — we're protected!

"This is something, when revival comes, that we will sense again. They sensed it in the early days of our country. They claimed the protection of the Lord, and they knew it day by day, every passing moment."

"People need to be educated on how to protect themselves in this time of evil," Geneva says. "Too many people don't know that."

"It's one of the things that we teach in this school of prayer," Gordon says. "That and the unseen personalities. In Wheaton, what they are afraid of is not people, but because of their lack of teaching or willingness to accept teaching on this subject, what they are really afraid of is the unseen personalities that foment evil within people. For years we've had situations that were totally impossible, and yet the spirit of God has protected us."

Another change in American life that Gordon expects is a shift in the job of schools. He thinks they will become "Sources of the promotion of righteousness."

How can that be, considering the legal obstacles established by courts?

"In this revival that is going to be coming, the whole legal system is going to change," Gordon says. "We can change any law we want. There is such a thing as repeal and even impeachment of Supreme Court justices. I think we are on the verge of some surprises. I am expecting that righteousness will take over for a period of time.

"The situation will get worse and worse in parts of the world, but this revival will hit a major portion of the world so the church will be ready for the rapture, and there will be multitudes coming into the fold. So we'll have the two going side by side: evil and good.

"During the next revival, there will be so many converts, that it will affect politics. People will not tolerate politics as usual, where leaders can lie one minute and backpedal the next."

"I think there will be great persecution, too," Geneva says. "The persecution might be because our political people have not taken that stance as those who are really willing to put their neck on the line. As it has been in other countries, we haven't experienced that in the U.S. ... renounce your Christian faith, or you're gone."

"I see in this next revival whole cities that will be in darkness because they have been headed that way, and because of rejection of the light," Gordon says. "I see whole cities that will be accepting the gospel as well. That wouldn't be everybody, but generally."

Gordon and Geneva came away with some valuable lessons from the African revival they experienced. One of the greatest was seeing how it dissipated because of its rejection by other Christians.

"In the 1951 revival, as this revival started to cool down, some of us who had been there wondered, 'Why does this have to be? Why can't it continue?'" Geneva says. "One who came back from furlough really questioned the authenticity of what had happened and verbalized it. Many felt this kind of doubt is what really squelched it."

"Some people came back and asked, 'Where is this revival?' That was not the question to ask," Gordon says. "They should have asked, 'How can I engage in serious intercessory prayer,' because it was moving, like a spreading flame."

Thus, the biggest enemy is unbelief among some believers, rejection of the power of God by those who have been endowed with it through their acceptance of Jesus Christ.

Likewise, the greatest key to *starting* the flame of revival is prayer. The Bible says, and that missionary and African pastor demonstrated, that

> *If my people, which are called by my name, shall humble themselves, and pray, and seek my face, and turn from their wicked ways; then will I hear from heaven, and will forgive their sin, and will heal their land.* — II Chronicles 7:14

And the greatest key to *spreading* the flame of revival in America is personified in the witness of the littlest evangelist: newborn Susan Christensen, the baby who brought down walls of suspicion, distrust and prejudice in African villages, and helped villagers view Gordon and Geneva as friends.

"To me the basic plan of God for evangelism is called 'friendship evangelism'," Gordon says. "It is one of the most effective ways, because people are given the opportunity, which God wants, of looking in on your life, and your heart, and your family. ... I have told pastors over and over again, always make friends. Because God is going to arrange it so they will need help, and need it badly. And when they do, all they are going to think about is your name."

The next revival, they think, will spread from friend to friend, not from media event to media event. Building bridges between people, all kinds of people — family, fellow workers, neighbors — is laying the groundwork for God to move. Thus, all His children will have a role in winning the victory.

And it will be individuals who, instead of waiting for someone else to make it happen, humble themselves, and pray, and seek God, and turn from their wicked ways, that the flame of revival will ignite.

Chapter 8

Evelyn's Legacy

In April 1952, Gordon and Geneva left Africa for six months of language study in Belgium. It was clear to missions officials that they needed time to recover their health. Geneva had been on the field a little less than three years, had a life-threatening illness, had her first child, and had continued to doggedly push herself at the mission station. She had run herself ragged. Gordon also had endured much illness. In fact, he said "illness" summed up his impressions of that first term. It afflicted them mercilessly.

It was time to take a break — if raising a 1-year-old in a foreign culture in a tiny apartment full of heirloom antiques is any kind of respite. That was Geneva's lot, however.

The culture, for example, was harder for her to relate to than the African culture. Belgium in the 1950s had a spiritual coldness that chilled Geneva to the bone. Her words for Belgium in those days were "spiritual depravity." Even the church buildings — big, with cold stone walls, and attended by a few elderly women wearing black bonnets — offered no sense of welcome or comfort. In fact, the very first message they heard from the pulpit of the Methodist church they attended, because there were no Covenant churches in Belgium, was that Susan was not welcome in the fellowship and was not to be brought back. With no Sunday school or nursery available, that meant either Gordon or Geneva would have to sit out each service they attended to care for her.

Then there was the housing.

"We were going to live in a huge old mansion renovated into apartments," Geneva said. "We were in this madam's house, and we had this great big Louis Quatorze bed in the living room, and she had a big glass, beautiful cupboard with all this precious china and stuff, heirlooms from way back there, and we're moving in with this baby who wasn't even 1 year old."

The kitchen was like a dollhouse in size. It had several gas burners but no refrigerator, and one little sink that Geneva felt brought down the wrath of Madame whenever she used it.

"Almost every time I turned on the water, to wash out diapers or something because there was no washing machine, she would come running up the stairs. 'You Americans use too much water!'

"I was always petrified. What if Susan were to bang her fist into that glass china cabinet there? Then we had all the ancestors in huge pictures hanging all over the walls glaring down at us. And one day we came home from church, and Grandpa had fallen out of the frame. I said, 'Don't touch him. Let me get Madame. Because if you pick that up and the frame breaks or something, then there will be bad trouble.' I wasn't going to touch any of those things, because she was so bound up in ancestry. This had been true in Africa. And here, we had come into it again, even though they didn't exhibit it in the same ways. They were really bound up in it."

So "furlough" was not rest and relaxation. Nevertheless, there were good times. It wasn't long before another young couple, missionaries with the Free Church, moved in with their daughter, who was 1 month younger than Susan.

"It was cold when we came and no way to have any heat, then came the summer months, and it was very hot," Geneva said. "So we said, 'We've got to get a little refrigeration in here so we can keep some sweet milk for these kids.' So we asked Madame if it was all right if we bought a little 4-foot refrigerator. We installed it on the landing, and I had to stand on a chair to reach it from our kitchen. And our missionary friend could open a trap door at the big stairway landing and reach it halfway down the stairs. This was after World War II, and these trap doors and other structural changes were as they had them then. That house had housed officers, and there was a big bomb shelter in the back yard and all this.

"Anyway, we had to get a special meter to put on that little fridge, so we would be sure to pay the electricity that it used. That mentality seemed so ridiculous to me. Why not just add another dollar?

"But that refrigerator, and us jumping up and down from the chair getting our milk, I think it was just a pain to her. Of course, I can see where we were a pain to her anyway. We were young and having fun: we devised this string between our windows, their upper window and our lower window, and put a bell at the top and a bell at the bottom, so if we wanted to talk to each other, we'd go pull the string and ring the bell, and hang out the window. And Madame would say, 'Oh, these Americans!' She didn't know what to do with us.

"Anyway, then we got a bath once a week. We could not draw our own water. The bathroom was on the first floor, and she would run the bath water.

"If she had let us divide that bath water out over the week, it would have given us baths all week! But she had this mammoth — it was like a stock tank, almost — and she would run this thing full, then she would get on the telephone; every floor had a telephone. And you'd get, 'MR. CHRISTENSEN, YOUR BAAAATH,' she'd say. She sounded like a sheep to me. And we'd laugh. He'd go down and take his bath. And she'd run my bath water. Well, first I would sponge Susan off real good, because I'd just sponged her off in the little basin. Then I took our laundry, and we washed our laundry in there afterwards, and then we'd take it up and string it all over.

"This was the kind of thing that made me think, 'Oh, in Africa I had the freedom.' We had water, although it was carried with difficulty from the spring, but we had water, and I didn't have anybody on my case all the time."

* * * *

They had been in Belgium about one month when tragic news arrived from the Congo: Geneva's sister Evelyn had been killed.

One morning she had gone over to the little mission school between 6 and 6:30. She had gotten a Bible verse for the day written on the board:

> *Keep thy heart with all diligence; for out of it are the issues of life.* — Proverbs 4:23

As a storm was rolling in, she had gone over by the window to sit at one of the children's desks to work on lesson plans.

She was struck by lightning as she sat there. The bolt had apparently traveled through the wiring for the lights, a shoddy job with lights tacked to the ceiling and wiring tacked to trees, through a lightbulb and struck her in the temple.

When the children arrived for school and she wasn't at the door to greet them, they knew something was wrong. They looked in and saw only her foot, while her body lay slumped at the desk. They ran screaming to Elmer Pearson's house for help.

There was nothing that could be done. The next day the missionaries had a funeral at the mission station, attended by the villagers, Belgian and Portuguese officials in the region, and missionaries from the Free Church. The service was given that day in French, Lingala and Ngbaka, "So the Word got out that day," Geneva says. "A very positive message."

After the service, Evelyn's body was buried at the Karawa post cemetery, where several other missionaries and children have been laid to rest.

Evelyn's brief term in the Belgian Congo had far-reaching consequences, however. She had been the first teacher to ever go on the Covenant field for the express purpose of teaching and helping the missionary children. She had had difficulty finding sponsorship for her work, because many churches did not view it as true missionary work. One church had withdrawn its support when it found out what she would be doing, and the second church sponsored her reluctantly.

In her time as the teacher there, she had been holding classes in what had been a storeroom. One of her jobs each day was to shovel ant hills out of the place.

After her death, the work of missionary teachers was never questioned again, Geneva says. It has always been funded since. Memorial funds in Evelyn's name came to the mission, paying for the first segment of the missionary school that now stands at the Karawa mission station. Two teachers, a Free Church member and a Covenanter, responded to the call to take Evelyn's place, and the educational work has been growing since.

Evelyn's life and time in Africa were short. But she appears to have accomplished much in that brief time — more than she probably expected to accomplish by age 29, and having spent one year as a missionary.

* * * *

After six months in Belgium, Gordon and Geneva left for the U.S. in November 1952. The return home was a wonderful opportunity to see Geneva's family again. They stayed with Geneva's parents in Kansas, who finally got to meet Susan. And there was time to sort through the tragedy of Evelyn's death.

However, "furlough" doesn't really mean rest. Gordon and Geneva spent much of their time driving, on a bus or train to wherever the World Missions headquarters sent them to speak to churches.

"On that home assignment we basically spent our time living with the folks between itineration trips," Geneva says. "We were in the Chicago missionary apartments for a few weeks, too. The folks gave us the largest bedroom in their two-bedroom house, because we had the baby. Of course, I thoroughly enjoyed being home on the farm, and Gordon was very much at home, too. Susan loved the dog, cats and patting the cows and horses as they ate in the manger. My folks were wonderful hosts, but I realize now it was quite an imposition on them."

Gordon and Geneva also served as staff for Covenant Bible summer camps — she as camp nurse and he as a missionary speaker and Bible teacher. Gordon had been sick much of the time.

During one of the itineration trips, to Topeka, Kansas, Geneva and a friend were shopping in a store when she was summoned to the telephone. The message: Gordon had suffered an apparent heart attack! He was 28. She rushed to the hospital where Gordon had been admitted.

"He was in the hospital for several days, and then with friends until he was stronger," Geneva says. "We went back to the farm, and the Mission Office in Chicago requested us to go there for a complete checkup at Swedish Covenant Hospital."

At Swedish Covenant doctors determined that Gordon had collapsed from a bad case of amoebic dysentery and exhaustion.

There was more shocking news to arrive that year — news that so rattled Geneva that her first thought was, "The Lord has really made a mistake." The Mission Council, which directed placement and missionary emphasis, was asking them to do a job they had never done before. Their assignment was changing upon their return to Africa. The board wanted them to go to the Bible Institute of the Ubangi as instructors.

LIFE LESSONS

The six months in Belgium marked the end of Gordon and Geneva's first term as missionaries. When Gordon looks back on those years he sees it as preparation for what was to come. The real work had not yet begun.

To describe that time in two or three words, he would use "illness" and "language."

Practice with French, Lingala and the tribal language of Ngbaka as well as the introduction to village missionary work all laid a groundwork with a value that could not be estimated at the time. But it was done in the face of much sickness, a nagging distraction, a personal reason for never doing what they came to Africa to really do.

"People have often asked, 'Why didn't you quit?'" Geneva says. "Well, God kept opening doors for us to go back. I feel that it all has been a training process."

That training process included accepting the responsibilities of family and working as a team. For Geneva, that transition was "a humbling process, but a very blessed one."

"I was a very independent person when we got married, but I saw that had to change," she says. "I believe God's desire was for us to minister to families, and that required being a family. To minister to wives, I needed to walk that path. The same is true of the men and Gordon."

Walking that path soon opened her eyes to deeper understanding of life in Africa. "We were out in the villages and saw these poorly trained village preachers and their wives, who had no training. My question at that time was, 'What can we do to help those women?' But I never expected to be the one to have to figure that out! I was hoping someone else would come and pick up this ball and run with it. But as it happened, on our first furlough, we got word that they wanted us to go to the Bible Institute the next term and teach. And

I thought, 'The Lord has really made a mistake, because I don't know anything about this.' But in seeing this need at that time, it was that which set the stage for me to be willing to make some drastic changes in what I thought my missionary work was going to be. That first term just changed that. And I praise the Lord that He helped me understand that you don't go out with a mindset that 'Either I do this or I am bound, I can't serve the Lord.' He made me flexible enough to see that He was unfolding and opening new doors.

"I guess that was what was really accomplished that first term to enable me to go on to further ministry. And I enjoyed it a lot."

Chapter 9

Into The Classroom

When Gordon and Geneva began their second missionary term at the Bible Institute in Tandala, neither of them felt they were the "teacher types."

"We had no formal training, except maybe a Christian education course at North Park," Gordon says. "But this moved us completely out of our comfort zones, which for me was preparing messages and delivering them, and for Geneva was the practice of medicine."

They were also stepping into an area that had seen one problem after another. The institute had been founded in 1949 with 12 African men who were veterans of missionary work and had received about two years of formal training themselves. They saw the great value in education. Will Norton of the Free Church, who went on to become a professor at Wheaton, was the first instructor. Sig Westberg, Monroe Sholund and the Dick Andersons followed him into the work during those most difficult founding days.

"The devil withstood that school," Geneva says. "They tried and tried for years to get this thing going. And no matter how they worked at it, sickness, one thing after another delayed it."

When Gordon had first arrived in Africa, the school had actually stopped classes, and Dick Anderson had taken the students out do do practical work in the field. Those students where on the field, therefore, when the revival came in 1951, and Geneva says "they were used mightily of God."

The sweep of that revival went far beyond the area of the mission and really riveted people's attention on the things of God. "So all these delays, even though the devil seemed to be keeping the school shut down in many ways, yet God in his own way was doing other work." The far-reaching effects of that revival were the best advertising the school could ever have. Eager students from throughout that part of Africa came seeking knowledge on how they could become pastors and enter the work.

The school at Tandala started on a Free Church mission station. It was about 110 miles from Karawa, where Gordon and Geneva had been based their first term. The school was housed in a building that Will Norton and a crew of African workers had constructed of giant beams they had hewn out of the jungle, beams the size of railroad bridge trestles. The walls were brick that had been fired on the construction site, and the roof was straw.

Tandala was a developing station. It had schools for children, but the big thing was the Bible Institute. Work was also under way on a hospital, overseen by Dr. Titus Johnson, who had come into that area with the Free Church in 1923 and was back to help the church expand its medical work.

One of the biggest problems, again, was health.

"The drainage system was such that the garden runoff came down to where we got our drinking water," Geneva says. "We boiled our drinking water, but you can't even wash your face sometimes without getting a bit of amoebic dysentery. Whatever you touched. Aemobic dysentery was so rampant there that we had a lot of illness."

The school also was far from a finished work. Their first year there, Gordon and Geneva were developing curriculum as they went, usually about a day ahead of the class.

"It was Mickey Mousing all the way for me, and for Geneva, of course, she had to establish courses," Gordon says. "Sigurd Westberg had started certain courses, and he had mimeographed materials and I think he had gotten up to and finished the Pentateuch. So now we were going to start with Joshua. Then from there on I had to make up my own lesson plans and very often we didn't have good materials or good machines, so we spent that first year inching our way through how to prepare a curriculum.

Geneva also was preparing her own curriculum, and was realizing how much God had prepared her for her new assignment during her first term.

"When we went to Tandala, that was a big time of being out of my realm of experience and knowledge. When they put us there, I thought, 'Lord, does this match up with what I saw last term?' and felt there had to be some help for these women to prepare them to be pastors' wives. And I thought, 'If we are going to be here, I've got to do something to develop a school for these women,' because we did not have a school at that time."

What Geneva had seen on her first term was that African pastors would not only need a thorough knowledge of the Bible, but also they were going to need to challenge their cultural standards with biblical standards and rethink their attitudes about women. Women were held in such low esteem that they were expendable. Unwanted wives could be thrown out on a whim. Their function was to have children and do hard labor. These were the lessons both men and women had been taught since childhood. By the time they were adults, women were serving their husbands meals, then going to sit and look at a wall; a wife was deemed so low, she wasn't even fit to see her husband eat. If he needed something, he would call her to the table, then she'd go back to look at the wall.

Geneva saw that they would have to come to regard each other as brothers and sisters in Christ, one flesh, partners in the work.

But how do you do that? She had seen the problem during the first term and thought about it. She had hoped someone else would step in and handle this; she didn't feel capable.

But it was as if God had shown it to her the first term, then changed her assignment so she could work on fixing it.

"I thought, 'If we're going to be here, I've got to do something to develop a school for these women.' ... But I had no teaching experience, I had no idea what their needs were. I'd go sit with them in the village, observe them, and they would come to me with their problems and so forth. So all of my lesson preparation was built around, 'What does Scripture have to say about their needs?'"

There was a huge obstacle in this at first for Geneva. While she started to build a rapport with the women in their own setting, once she started to offer formal classes, they suddenly cooled toward her. In fact, she felt almost as if she were being shunned.

"When I would pass them in the palm lane, they would look the other way," Geneva says. "They would not have anything to do with me. This really troubled me, because I thought, 'Lord, what am I going to do? I didn't know what the problem was. I prayed about it, and I remember even asking the Lord to change the color of my skin if that would help. I was just desperate about it. I prayed about it. Wept about it. And I thought, 'Lord, you have opened up this door to be here now, but I can't seem to get anybody to go through that door.'"

The frustration lasted six months.

"When they were absent, I would go right down to the village after class, and I would say, 'I'm so sorry you're sick and couldn't be in class,' and I always worked on the premise that they had a very good excuse. I never scolded them for it. And they would be quite embarrassed. They would be sitting there pounding their corn and so forth. Physically they were rejecting the idea of class."

Then, suddenly, that rejection ended. They were so intent on coming that they would even come when they shouldn't, and Geneva would have to send them home because they were sick.

Geneva finally asked one of the students about the turnaround.

"'Oh Mama,'" Geneva recalls her saying, "'when you said you were going to have class for us so we could learn and be helpers together with our husbands, we thought you had an ulterior motive. We couldn't imagine something like this would be done just for us women. Because they always say we are mpamba (PAH mba, meaning worthless).'

"These women viewed themselves as being the workhorse in the family and the one to produce children. But as a worth to any other degree, they couldn't accept the fact that they were a worthy person, to even have a class like that. So we worked on that a lot. I said, 'Don't ever let me hear you say that word, that you are a mpamba woman. God never made a worthless thing, and He made you.' So we had a lot of things like that to work on.

"But they said, 'When we saw that you would come and sit with us at night in our sickness, and were up all night delivering our babies, and you left your own family home, we realized you really meant what you said. You wanted to help us. Now we want to cooperate and be a part of that.'

"And that," Geneva says with a laugh, "is how the Lord overcame that without changing the color of my skin."

The lesson topics were often on daily living. Geneva was able to combine her medical training with her lessons.

"We realized we had to start from the ground up and build into them hygienic principles too, and hygiene was one of our big classes."

Lesson One in disease control was digging a hole and building a "cabinet," or outhouse. Then came physical hygiene.

"I would start out by bringing the microscope to class, and we would take water from one of their fingers before it was washed and look at it — pretty gross. Then I'd have them wash with soap real well and put a drop under there — oh my, that's much better. And so the first thing we would learn was to wash our hands in a wash basin, using soap, throw that water out and have that ready for somebody else.

"Each lesson we had in hygiene, they had to add to their lifestyle. Later I'd go around and do inspections.

"We did all of these things. We'd even get down to having a bowl of flowers on the table. We went beyond strictly hygiene to neatness and appearance of the home.

"We had been doing this for several years, and I got so weary of going around inspecting everything from the john house on. This year I thought, 'They have come far enough. They are doing a real good job of this.'

"The men came after a few weeks, and they said, 'Mama, when are you going to start peeteune?'

"I wondered, 'What in the world is this peeteune?' and I didn't want to embarrass them by not understanding the word they were using, so I said, 'Just tell me a little more. I must be neglecting something. Can you tell me a little more about what you want me to do?'

"'When you come around and look at everything to be sure it is in order in our houses.'

"Ohhh. So they were using the French word 'inspection,' and it came out 'peeteune.' I said, 'Well, I thought your wives were doing such a good job, I didn't think it was necessary anymore.'

"'Oh, no. We want you to tell them, do peeteune every week.' So then, what I did was train an African to go with me, and then sometimes I wouldn't go at all.

"It was things like that. It had been a slow process of learning. I think what we learned was, what you teach in the classroom you don't leave it there, hoping that maybe it will soak in. Maybe they will do it. No. Immediately I expected that to be done, and we made provisions for it, show them how it could be done in their homes."

These were the easy lessons, and only the beginning. The Africans suffered not only from numerous diseases, but they suffered from unbiblical relationships and ways of life. These took as heavy an emotional and mental toll on them as disease took physically.

The key tool for this job was not soap or a microscope, but the Bible. Geneva took these women into the Bible daily, and in doing so was surprised to see how much more this book had to offer than even she had realized. All her childhood years of memorizing verses and family devotionals and study paled compared to how the book was opening up to her now. She realized it was deeper and richer than she had ever imagined, and all her past study seemed to have only familiarized her with it.

"We didn't want to do anything that was culturally damaging, but if the culture dictated things that were ungodly, unholy, then it had to be dealt with," Geneva says. "But let the Word of God deal with it as much as possible. So that's the premise that I've tried to work with. And to me, I got more and more excited about the Bible. I hardly knew a thing about it before. To realize how it speaks to the needs of people, to their hearts — the Bible became much more alive as I was teaching it to them. And I saw it speaking to their needs."

The challenges were constant, however, and Geneva had to look to the Lord directly to overcome some of the obstacles she faced. For example, how do you get a thought like, "For God so loved the world, that He gave His only begotten son," to come alive for people who have no concept of love and do not even have a meaningful word for God's kind of love in their vocabulary? Love was not a factor in marriage. Love was not a factor between the husband and wife. Love, the foundational motivation of the Bible, was absent, period.

"We were having class one day ... and I was trying to explain to them what the love of God is like," Geneva says. "I was grappling, groping for some example. How do you convey love? And I knew this would never convey to them the idea of love, but I asked them, 'Why did your husband marry you?'

"'So he'd have somebody to cook for him and wash his clothes.'"

"'Why did Nzambwa (Gordon) marry me?'"

"'So he'd have somebody to care for him.'"

She was getting nowhere. Then she noticed Alliete sitting in the front row, holding her 6-month-old child. She had waited 20 years to have a child. All the joy in her life was now in her arms.

"I looked at her and I know the Lord had to have told me to do this, inspire me," Geneva says. "I said, 'Alliete, go out and throw little Melices out in the jamba, out in the woods.' And she looked at me as if I had gone stark crazy. All the women gasped. This missionary lady telling her to go throw her baby out there? She just clung to that little baby and said, 'I will *never* do that.'"

"I said, 'Why not?' And then she started to tell us what her feelings were for that little baby.

"Then I said, 'Okay, now can you get the idea of how God loves us? That's what that word means.' Then they all went, 'Oohhhh.'

"We know God's love is far beyond that, but that helped them get the concept of love. And it's this kind of teaching concept that we had to be looking for all the time."

Among the cultural values they challenged was the disunity of their families. First, marriages usually had been arranged between the parents of the bride and groom, and their feelings toward each other were not a factor. This was a business deal, about money and payments and dowries. It was in many ways like the purchase of a slave for a man. Then, in contrast to God's command that "two will become one flesh," the husband and wife would stay separate, even at meal time.

So there was often great enmity between husband and wife, particularly among wives who had become bitter.

Geneva said that on her early visits with African women, she would be so horrified by the way women would speak about their husbands that it would nearly turn her stomach. Women working together, preparing food or washing clothes, would hatefully rip their husbands to shreds, discussing every disparaging aspect of their lives with the other women.

Yet to the men's faces, the women needed to be respectful, subservient, because a husband could simply throw a wife out if he wanted. Or get a second wife he found more likable and make the first wife even more the family workhorse. She could be beaten and bullied with no social protection. She felt constantly threatened.

Thus families seemed deeply split and unstable. Except for the few strands of expedience that held them together, couples were usually quite distant.

The culture perpetuated this as well. First of all, the marriage dowry had become the biggest financial deal families ever made. It lead to daughters practically being auctioned off. It also meant that a common man might have to pay in installments, keeping him indebted to his in-laws forever. And any late or missed payments brought the wrath of the in-laws down on the man, and could even lead to them "repossessing" the woman until the man came up with the money.

Secondly, an uncle was the traditional go-between for arranging a marriage. An uncle was considered close enough to the family to be trusted. Since an uncle picked out a man's wife, and that decision was based on wheeling and dealing rather than the best interests of the couple, it made it easier for a man to abandon his wife. When marriage difficulties arose, a husband could quickly point a finger at his family.

As Gordon describes it, a man would say, "I didn't choose this wife. Who was so stupid to choose this woman from the middle of the jungle (the worst curse of all, that her mother delivered her out in the jungle) and here I've got her?"

Perhaps the worst situation, however, was the endorsement of polygamy. That totally destabilized families.

It was a cudgel that kept women subservient because of the danger of being less favored, rather than rising to the level of co-laborer with a husband.

Yet Christianity is about unity and love. In particular, these traits had to be evident in ministry couples, the African pastors and wives Gordon and Geneva were supposed to be developing. Otherwise, these pastors would never succeed. How do you start instilling such counter-cultural concepts?

A little at a time. Gordon and Geneva saw that families seemed to stay split from each other at every turn, even at meal time.

"The men would eat separately, and the women ate separately," Gordon says. "Then they fed the kids, so there never was a time when the family ate together. So we decided they had to have some time when the family ate together. Whether they did it like we did it was immaterial. But they had to have a family time."

"We were trying to build a family relationship where the man would respect the wife and the wife would respect her husband," Geneva says.

"We consider that the family is the basic unit of society," Gordon says. "It is also the No. 1 problem of the African. Our emphasis in all of our years out there was, 'How do you help the family?' Because one family giving an example of a Godly family in the village was worth thousands and thousands of teachings."

"I used to tell the women before they would head out on internship — because they would have two years at the Bible Institute and then a year of internship — I'd say, 'Before you ever go out to beat that drum to gather the women together for a meeting, you live in that village with your husband and children, showing the kind of love that you have been taught here and that you exhibit here. Just go there and live as a family peacefully without shouting at your husband when he is halfway down the road, calling him names and yelling at the kids. Just go and live like Christians among them for awhile.' Then I said, 'If you even need to beat the drum, you'll have more women at that meeting than you can handle.'"

"And I'll never forget this one woman who came back and said, 'I did that and it was true. I had so many women coming to my door and asking me, 'How in the world can your family exist like this? You don't yell at each other, you work together with your husband. Your husband seems to respect you.' And there she had all the opportunity she could use to talk to them and tell them, 'It's because of Jesus in our hearts.'"

These changes, however, did not occur unchallenged. One of Geneva's means of defense was her teapot. She says she often saw trouble coming down the road and put on a pot of tea so she could soften up an angry person by offering him a nice, fresh cup of tea.

"There were several things I almost got myself in trouble for at the time," Geneva says. One of the big ones was teaching women to sit on a chair. She had realized when women came to her home that they did not know how, let alone set any kind of table for a guest or have any kind of plan for hospitably greeting a visitor.

"So I was teaching them how to sit on a chair, and one day I see this whole entourage of men coming down the palm lane ... and I got the teapot on," she recalls with a laugh.

She invited them in, knowing something big was waiting. They finally got around to their purpose for coming.

"They said — one is always the spokesman and he started clearing his throat — 'Is it true that you are teaching our wives to sit on a chair?' I said, 'Oh yes. It is very true.'"

"'Why are you doing this? If you're going to teach them to sit on a chair, before we know it they're going to be take over the whole domain. And they're going to be bossing us around.'

"I said, 'Well, what is it you are here preparing to do?'

"'We are preparing to be pastors.'

"'Where are you going to be ministering?'

"'Well, we don't know. Some will be on mission stations, some will be in the village, some may even be in the towns.'

"I said, 'Now how would you like your wife to be able to perform if you have a guest in the house? You want her to cover her face and start laughing and run and hide in the cookhouse? Let's say you are not home, and you have guests come. What do you want you wife to be able to do? Do you want her to be able to offer that person a chair, so they can sit down? Would you like for her to be able to put a cup of tea in front of them in a dish and be something that you would approve of?'

"'Oh. We hadn't thought of that.'

"'What would you like for her to do, if somebody invites you to their place, as they are going to be doing, because,' I said, 'Congo is not standing still. This is a progressive country. You're going to be going places with your wives. Do you want them to sit at your feet on a stool when you go to somebody's house, or do you want them to sit on a chair? Do you want them to sit out in the kitchen and eat while you sit at the table and eat, or do you want them to be able to sit beside you and eat like the other people do?'

"'Oh. We've never thought of this.'

"'Well,' I said, 'These are the reasons I am teaching this. If your wives learn how to do this, they are not going to try to take over your whole house.' Then we went through the whole matter of if the husband loves his wife as himself, he is not going to throw her out at night, so she ends up on my doorstep in the morning, but he is going to want her to progress at the rate he is.

"We'd have long sessions. And they went out of there so happy. It was just a whole new concept, but we had to build this concept into the men, too."

So while Bible teaching was a big part of the curriculum, Gordon and Geneva also put a lot of work into stabilizing family lives. As she said, often these men, on track to be pastors and Christian role models, were still throwing their wives out when they got mad at them. She found one of her best tools for overcoming this was a can of sardines.

"That first term, I don't know why I ordered a whole case of sardines ... but I used more sardines to help families build their relationships back up. I don't know how many times I would get up in the morning, and there sat a woman outside who had been cast out of her home in the night. Now these were pastors and their wives training to go out as pastors, but that was the worth of a woman, and if he didn't like what she did that day, out the door she went, and he shut the door on her.

"I asked her, 'What would your parents have done? What was the thing you learned from your culture if you were cast out as a wife?' And I'll never forget, this one lady told me, 'They would give us a duck if they had it or a chicken, and send us back home and say, 'You go prepare that the best way you know how for your husband, and show him kindness.' Love was not even in their vocabulary. Show him kindness.

"So I said, 'All right, that's what we'll do then. I have sardines,' and they loved them. So that's where the sardines came in. And I would send them back to the house with a can of sardines ... they had the roots to go with it. I said, 'Go back and do the nicest cooking you know how for your husband, even though he threw you out last night. And see what affect it has.' Well, this began to just pull them in, you know.

"Sometimes the men would come and say, 'I have this impossible woman.' And often we would ask, 'Who chose her? Did you choose this wife?'

"'No ... It is not the one I wanted to marry anyway.'

"'Well,' I'd say, 'Do you believe that the Lord Jesus Christ has transformed you when you received Him as your savior?

Do you believe you were a sinner and he made you into a saint? Do you believe he is able to do that?' Oh yeah, as far as their salvation was concerned, they were sure God could do that. I said, 'Do you believe God can give you love for that woman?'

"'Oh, no. Never.'

"'Well,' I said, 'if God can save you, I think He can give you love for that woman.' And I would say the same thing to the woman.

"I said this was a matter of entrusting this to God's hands, and we can see Him do a miracle here in your married life as He did in your soul. And we saw time and again, some of those early people who came to us have the strongest marriages, because they learned that doing for one another what they would have done unto them, they could build a relationship that eventually led to real love."

Gordon and Geneva have one memory that showed this taking place. Upon graduation of their 1955 class, the church decided that pastors and wives should have a Christian wedding before going onto the field. Some of these couples already had six children, but there they stood, solemnly exchanging vows.

Yet one of the students, Doko, did an unusual thing. He took his wife by the hand, which was almost never done in public, and he said, "Rebecca is my wife. I love her, and I am going to love her until we die." And he did, Gordon and Geneva say, until Rebecca's death many years later. That moment in the wedding ceremony was a confirmation for Gordon and Geneva that love was coming alive in the hearts of these people.

Relationships with children were also very unloving and often cruel. One of the traditions of the people Gordon and Geneva worked with were called "Gaza" camps for adolescents. Children nearing puberty would leave the home for a year in the jungle camp. If a child had been deemed incorrigible by the parents, the camp leader, who was appointed by the village, would be instructed to whip him into shape. And this he did, almost literally, with a year's worth of severe beatings that could kill a child.

It was not uncommon for a child to die during that year, but parents were never informed until the camp ended. They would find out the morning the camp was released. If the grass crown had been removed from the point of their roof during the night and placed in their doorway, it signaled that their child had died at camp. Women would dread going out of their houses on the day the camp was over.

The camp was for learning folklore and getting instruction in how to be a man or woman. But Gordon said the two greatest evils of the camps were the brutality and the worship rites.

"They had what was called the Gaza pole, and this stick was to represent the tribal deity," Gordon says. "At a point in the camp, they would cut both the boys and girls — in the boys in was circumcision, and in the girls it was concision — and they would take the blood from this surgery and they would offer it to this Gaza stick. When you look at it, the idol was a representation of Satan, and it was a dedication of their bodies to Satan.

"So when people ask us, 'Was there anything like Satanism over there?' that was all there was. When missionaries went over there, it was a question of helping them see they were worshipping Satan, and that they could turn to worshipping God."

Geneva says that also one of the worst things they did to the children was teach them to be deceptive.

"Can you imagine working with a people who have been taught to be deceptive? We had more problems with this. If they can get away with it, they are the winner. If they can't then they have to admit it was bad. But if they can get away with it, there's no sin in it. You're dealing with people who say, 'Hey, I got away with that so it's all right. God doesn't look at that as sin.' The first time some of the people were hearing the story of the crucifixion and Judas, they said, 'Hey, Judas was the hero!' Until he hanged himself."

"The people's folklore is representative of a people's attitude and mindset," Gordon says. "All of their folklore, whether it's this little mousedeer that deceives an elephant or this little spider that deceives an antelope or something like that, deception is at the core of it. So when the gospel came, it was head-on with everything that was wrong, evil, unhealthy, disreputable."

The people also lived under an array of superstitions and taboos that held them in bondage. Women who heard birds singing first thing in the morning were under a curse, according to tradition, so the villages would pound drums first thing in the morning to drown out the sounds of birds. Men who received something with one hand instead of two were under a curse for violating that taboo. These culturally inflicted restraints could cripple individuals with fear for a lifetime.

But it took time for the people to let go of such traditions as the camps, or the taboos, or even carving markings into their bodies. While the missionaries reasoned with the people out of the scriptures, the missionaries also felt the pressure of criticism from social experts in their own culture — sociologists and anthropologists — that they were somehow violating these people by imposing foreign standards on them.

Social pressure is very hard. Whether it is people refusing for the first time to go to the camps, or missionaries facing criticism from the intelligentsia of their culture. But they both endured it, because they both had decided to adhere to God's teachings in the Bible.

Geneva remembers the concerns of the women in her Bible Institute women's courses as young people reached the age for camp.

Often the adult students with babies would bring babysitters of age 10 to 14 to help during class.

"These young girls would say they were getting pressure, especially from grandmothers, but mothers too, that when they got back they were going into the puberty rite camp. They would ask, 'What are we going to do? We don't believe that is right anymore.'

"I said, 'Sit down, and tell me exactly what they do and why you think it would be wrong to do it. We have to have some reason for you saying no to them.' They sat with me, a whole group, and they started telling me everything. And I said, 'Give me a few days and I am going to look in the scripture and see if I find anything that says this is not good.' For instance, there was a lot of alcohol consumption, and (after camp) they would grease these girls up, braid money into their hair, and they'd go around doing these sensuous dances, and it brought glory to Grandma. It was a second time for Grandmother to be in the limelight, and she loved it. Then they would get money when they went around and did these things.

"Did the Lord have anything to say about this kind of thing? I went right down the line, one point after another. I went to the scriptures and found where it is said, then I called them back over one day and said, 'This is what God says.'"

Geneva also discussed medical aspects, with Dr. Teddy Johnson giving them information. Though they might only be babysitters for the actual students, these girls had to learn to read while at the school, and the lessons were written down for them to review.

"When they went home, they could put their arm around their mother or grandmother, whoever was pressuring them, and talk about it. Many of these adults said they were Christians, and it really got results. The grandmothers backed off."

It was a great joy to Geneva, seeing these girls delivered from a lot of pain, danger and error.

But in respecting the culture, "If God's word didn't have anything to say to it, then we felt we really didn't have anything that we could say to it, either," Geneva says. "Because our teaching has to have a reason for it."

That meant saying nothing when a woman might come to church nursing a baby monkey, Gordon says. It happened. "When it was through, it would jump around the church. But there is nothing in the Bible that says a mother can't nurse a monkey."

That baby monkey was usually going to end up a meal. It's mother had probably been killed for food by village hunters, and this baby was being fattened up for slaughter. "Everything is utilitarian out there," Gordon says.

The Lord also, however, was helping them with the pragmatic problems as well as the deep, fundamental ones. For example, there was the seemingly minor "status problem" of the Bible Institute in the eyes of other Bible schools in Congo. The Bible Institute had been on and off for six years, from 1949 to 1954, as it faced many obstacles.

One problem was family visitors hanging around with students in class and even living at school with them.

All these problems started to be solved. "After March of 1954, the school has run consecutively without any breaks," Geneva says. "But until that time, from about 1949 until 1954, it was one thing after another hindering. So the first graduating class was in 1955. There were 12 men and 12 women. We had the women's school running parallel to the men's school. So after that, more professors were added, and we had to move the school in 1958. It was moved to a new site that was independent of any other station. Because the students had so many relatives and friends coming, hindering them from doing their studying when they were on the station, we went to an independent place and made some firm rules about people coming. They couldn't come and stay like that. They needed more garden space and a better water system. And the school has progressed to the point now where the Bible Institute has become a theological school. ... it is an accredited theological training school."

"It is one of nine superior theological schools in Zaire," Gordon says.

"We have the second largest and best library, if you can imagine that. ... That is where the school has gone. Now we have a Bible Institute that is not on the same level as the institute that we were teaching in, but it is an upgrade from the three-year Bible school."

The school was relocated to a place called Goyongo, independent of all stations. It was 99.2 hectacres of jungle.

Back in 1954, however, the Bible Institute was of no reputation. Gordon went to work on that with a tool he had become well acquainted with in the States — music. He started a band. It harkened back to his days as a student at North Park, or at Covenant churches during school breaks.

Gordon figured the Bible Institute could become unique and get some standing by not only being a pastors training site, but also for introducing musical instruments.

"For a while, I thought this would be the bane of us all, " Geneva recalls with a laugh.

Gordon had his trumpet, so he started teaching a man to play. They also had Geneva's accordion, given to her when she went on the field and had tried to practice on her way over on the ship to start her first term. So Gordon started teaching another man how to get some music out of it.

"It made a funny looking group," Gordon says.

But it was the beginning of a band, a project that grew. The institute eventually obtained used brass instruments from the States, and the band became a big extracurricular project for Gordon.

Before long, whenever a state official visited the area, he wanted the Bible Institute's band to come in. They learned to play the national anthem, but from then on, it was "Onward Christian Soldiers" and "Stand Up For Jesus" and the rest of an evangelical repertoire.

There came a point in Zaire's unstable political history where the government decreed no more religious expressions in public.

"But (the government) had no other choice. The Goyongo Band was the only one, and they were leading the processions," Gordon says, laughing. So like it or not, when they called the band, they got Christian music for their parade through the area or to greet dignitaries.

The band also did its job of elevating the Goyongo Bible Institute out of second-class status. The band made a much more profound impact on the lives of its members as well. It taught a lesson about hope, planning and working for the future. This was a key lesson.

All these milestones, however, were reached from a day-to-day existence dogged by sickness again. Gordon and Geneva seemed to be constantly fighting illness, and, sometimes, the temptation to quit.

There were many discouraging times, "especially when we had the normal burdens of missionary work and also have the crisis times with our children," Gordon says.

One point in particular came in their second term, when Susan, near age 3, developed blackwater fever.

"Very few ever live through it," Geneva says. "When we came back that term, she could not get readjusted with malaria, and no matter how faithful we were with the anti-malarial medicine, the poor little thing would go into convulsions, and I would have to keep injectable quinine handy. ... It was a very strenuous time. I was pregnant with Michael at the time and we had gone up to my brother and his wife, who had come onto the field and they were in a remote area where buffalo hunting was good, and we needed meat. So we combined a visit with them, getting meat and an evangelism trip all at one time. We took Susan, and I carried my canning equipment to can meat. While we were there, I woke up this morning, and she went to the potty and it was black. And I knew. She had been feverish in the night.

They call it blackwater fever because the red corpuscles burst, and when they come out through the urine they turn black.

"That was frightening, because I knew there was not a lot of hope. So here I was trying to can my buffalo meat, and running back and forth between her crib and the cookhouse, and I was really stressed out.

"And finally the message got through to me from the Lord, 'Just commit her into My hands and trust Me, because this is something you cannot do anything about.'

"I remember getting down on my knees on that cement floor and saying, 'Lord, it is true. It is beyond us. And I commit her back into your hands.' And then I was able to finish my canning.

"But she did not get better. We talked to the doctor on the radio ... and he said, 'Well, medically there is nothing to do, just try to keep her comfortable, try to keep her temperature down, give her fluids to drink.' Then we had to go back to Tandala, so we traveled back with her. And for 10 days she just hung in the balance.

"I remember one night waking up when somebody died on the station and the whole town goes out wailing and crying, and in my subconscious mind — I was totally exhausted because I had been up with her and had the medical needs of the other people around me — and in my mind I thought, 'Oh, she's gone.' And I had put her crib beside my bed so I could just put my hand on her when she was restless, and I realized, no, she was still alive. It was somebody else.

"It was a hard time. One night she hemorrhaged through her mouth and nose, and her little bed was soaked, about half of it, and I thought, 'Oh no. It is getting so difficult.' And then our doctor there — we talked to our Covenant doctor in Karawa, and I said, 'Can you come over. I don't know what else to do. I wonder if we could transfuse her.' ... So Dr. Clitus Olson came over and said, 'I would never try to transfuse her. She is too fragile.'

"She looked like a little porcelain doll without any blood left in her. So we did as we had been, we kept praying. And that day was the last day she had any outburst of the broken cells. And she started recuperating, which was an absolute miracle.

"The poor little thing emotionally was just drained. We had to keep her by our bed for a long time. Her little nerves were so fragile. In her feverish times she would hallucinate and see these things. She would talk to us about it and everything. It took a long healing process for her."

With a laugh, Geneva adds, "And then it wasn't too long after that that she got her baby brother. So we had a busy time that term.

"But with each of our kids, we got to the point somehow where we were hopeless, the medical field was hopeless, and we had to say, 'Lord, they are back in your hands totally. We take our hands off.' So we know what it's like. But He spared all three of them."

What was the antidote to such pressure? What kept them coming back to missionary work in Africa? A big factor was the day-to-day excitement of being in the Word of God as a teacher, and seeing the light turn on in students.

"There were times when I was so excited about what I was about to teach, and then I'd go into the classroom and the students would get excited, then they would go out and share with others," Gordon says. "Love for the Word. Sharing the blessings of the Word. This is contagious. ... The work in the second term was a sheer delight, but physically we were always in trouble."

Geneva says, "Our story is not too different from others. They may not have had the extent of illness we had, but they felt it wiser to stay home, which I have great respect for. Some people have said, 'Were you out of your minds to keep going back?' But you know, when I first went to the mission field, I said, 'Now I know this is cut and dried, I know what the Lord wants me to do with the rest of my life. It is to be a missionary.' Yet every time we have come home on furlough ... we have had to pray through this whole thing again. 'Lord, is it Your time and is it Your will that we go back to the field again?' It is not something you get a green light on once and for all, 'This is something you are going to do.' Every time, we've had to work through that because of circumstances that were surrounding us that made it appear as though maybe it was not the right thing."

LIFE LESSONS

When Gordon and Geneva look back over this time in their lives, they can see some great lessons that came out of their experiences.

- When we decide to serve the Lord, we are going to find ourselves "over our heads" in many situations. That's the place where our personal strength, knowledge and talent are insufficient for the challenge and the only way to win is through our faith in God. And when we pass through that deep water point, we come out on the other side even stronger in Christ, having relied on Him instead of ourselves. We are also then even more able to serve, because we have drawn closer to him and exercised His power in us rather than our own power alone.

We must persevere. As Paul wrote in Ephesians, "having done all, stand." We have to learn to hold our ground in the spiritual contest, to walk and not faint. This can only come with faith, the "deep water" faith that comes from wading in over our heads with Christ holding us.

We must remember that the miraculous is possible. The disbelief of the world will harangue us daily with the message: "God can't, God won't, God is not there," to discourage us from walking out with Him. If we do not recognize that God is working miracles, and God does bare his arm for us, we will avoid the darkness that God has called us to challenge and overcome.

- Our marriages can work. God has a high stake in them.

Gordon and Geneva discovered a great secret of the Kingdom, and a great point of attack by the enemy: personal relationships. This is almost like the germ in every mustard seed of faith that Christ said can move mountains. While with human eyes we would expect the devil to have much grander attack plans against humanity and be concentrating on such things as propelling a Hitler or Stalin to the top, Gordon and Geneva discovered that the attack on humanity is a trench warfare. Intent on taking one house at a time, the devil launches an inch-by-inch assault on the soul with a much fiercer determination than we would anticipate. He doesn't take potshots at our personal lives; this is his front line, and he will dedicate a lot of force to undermining a marriage. The devil will put much work into poisoning family relationships, especially marriages, and then other relationships; neighbor to neighbor, culture to culture.

The intensity can be shocking, and even more shocking if we have underestimated our potential impact on the devil's domain. But perhaps there is an analogy in the Bible: a mighty king, Herod, who unleashed his army in an attack on a toddler. His attack was fierce and ruthless, driven by his deep fear of the potential that child had to destroy him someday. Like a king afraid of a baby, the devil is deeply afraid of the Christ in you. And the way to disarm that is to destroy the closest interpersonal relationships on earth, husband and wife, and ultimately God and child of God.

- The greatest way to learn is teach. Despite many hardships faced in those days, Gordon and Geneva speak with enthusiasm about what happened in their lives then. They found the Bible opening up in a thrilling way as they dedicated themselves to sharing it with others. The floodgates of understanding opened as they shared with others, as if suddenly coming up on a Grand Canyon vista. The Bible became a breathtaking adventure and a wonder to behold. The key to getting there was accepting responsibility to teach others.

What were the incidents that taught these lessons? Let's hear their own words.

On being over our heads:

"I found this testimony I had written while at North Park, ready to go out," Geneva says. "I was anticipating washing the lepers' sores and all this kind of thing. I don't know if I ever washed a leper's sores. ... It would have been much easier than to do what we were having to do, because I was always over my head, it seemed, in whatever it was I was doing. And this is another lesson I think I began learning there. Even though it appears the Lord is making a mistake sometimes, and He gets us into this water that is over our heads, He does not lead us in paths or ask us to do something where He will not supply either the wisdom or the grace or the way of escape. ... But it seemed like He was testing me along the way to see if I could really trust Him for the hard things. And I have learned. Or at least I'm still learning, I guess, that there's nothing too hard for the Lord. ... He will provide the way and the strength for us to call on, even though it might be hard. That is a wonderful thing to know."

On persevering:

"The greatest battle, spiritually, going on in the African Christians' lives is the battle against a happy, unified, God-glorifying Christian home," Gordon says. "If the enemy succeeds in the destruction of the testimony of a Godly home, he has virtually won the battle. We sought by means of marriage seminars, example and class teaching to help solidify Christian marriages."

On marriage:

"One thing I so often think of that I learned in our second term," Geneva says, "was that God can take a man and a woman who are totally miles apart, and if they are willing to commit themselves to one another and to grow in grace if not love, at that point, anyway, and to do for the other what they think would be pleasing and helpful to them, they can learn to love one another. ... I would often use the example of the garden when they would say, 'This (marriage) is impossible.' I would say, 'All right, when you plant your garden and just leave it there, what happens? It comes up, yeah. And if you don't go back and tend to it, what happens? You don't get any fruit. It dries up.'

"I said, 'the same thing happens to your marriage. You tend that every day. It's delicate. Very delicate.' ... I have since heard the African women preaching this same sermon, you know, because you can see a real likeness in that. And they learned that it is something you work at. That was a blessing to me."

Gordon says, "Another thing we learned in this process was that, as Geneva has already indicated, love is not an emotion. It is an act of the will. We don't get love out of the sky. Because some of these people had these marriages planned out for them by their families ... some of them were confident their families made a horrible choice. Nevertheless, when they realized that love is not an emotion. It is not some fuzzy thing, it is an act of the will, 'I WILL to do this good toward this person,' the will became the motor and the emotions became the caboose, instead of the other way around, which was how they in their original culture acted. And, of course, that is biblical, because if Jesus had depended on warm fuzzies toward us, He would never have gone to the cross. It was an act of the will."

"I'm afraid today we don't connect the scriptures as being a viable thing for us," Geneva says. "It is kind of discouraging sometimes to find that people don't take the promises of God as a personal thing and say, 'God, you said it, now I am claiming this promise for this situation.' I think we need to see more of that today. God didn't write His Word only for 2,000 years ago. He wrote it for us today just as much. ... Many times when the women were learning to read, they would ask me questions about cultural things I didn't know myself, so I'd say, 'All right, let's read this and you read it with me ... what do you think that says to your situation?' And I learned far more than they ever did, I'm sure, concerning God speaking to them in their particular situation."

"There was one other thing I was thinking when you talked about the miraculous," Gordon says. "Everything we did out there was a challenge. We were going to take a truck trip. The first truck that was ever committed to my care. I was the sole responsible party for it, and it was a truck that had a terrible radiator. It leaked and leaked and leaked. We had to be sure that we were going to be someplace where there were streams and be sure that water was accessible simply because it had to be filled up every once and awhile.

"So before we would start a trip, we would gather with the Africans to pray that God would take care of the tires and motor and everything. Here in the states, you know that there are gas stations, call boxes, and in Mexico, 'green angels.' The only green angels we had out there were jungles from which we could get vines and stuff to tie the truck back together again, which one time we certainly did. The drive shaft fell off, so we were grateful to be near a jungle and not a grassland, so that every few miles we could wrap it together and get on our way again.

"In America, we have created so many crutches and aids to life, and have so many services and so much high technology, that trusting God is not a part of our daily walk. We talk about it while relying on ourselves."

On learning through teaching:

"I really learned the Bible in Africa," Gordon says. "I learned ABOUT the Bible in seminary. But I really learned the Bible in Africa. And every class was a learning experience. I'm sure I must have learned half to two-thirds more than the students because it was so fascinating to pursue a topic or a cultural overhang that needed to be dealt with.

"After our first term, after our first home assignment, coming back was the teaching time. And that to me was the start of pay dirt for our growth spiritually, understanding the scriptures."

"It also set the tone for the next 20 years," Geneva says. "We had gone (to the Bible Institute) temporarily, because we said we did not feel we were teaching material, they had other missionaries that were better qualified. But as it turned out through circumstances and because we did enjoy it so much, they continued to call us back to the Bible Institute."

A Gift of Rain
A VIGNETTE

It was Wednesday, Nov. 30, 1994. Geneva was sitting at the kitchen table of her tidy home in a quiet, attractive retirement community on the Gulf Coast of Florida. She was now a retired missionary, retelling stories from long ago. There were so many. Her life obviously had been an adventure.

But of all the stories she had gathered in her life, one of her favorites seemed to be a story involving a Congolese pastor named Fiakona Jacob. As she told it, she would even offer her version of the dialog, turning the tale about a much-needed gift of rain into quite a drama.

The event occurred during the Christensen's fourth term, in the late '60s, at the Wasolo Mission Station.

"Working at Wasolo was very difficult," Geneva said. "We were alone and had no other missionaries to fellowship with. Our youngest daughter was still in high school, and that made it difficult for her, because we were so isolated. She didn't get to come home ever, unless it was for vacation.

"It was a hard term because there were a lot of testings. We were working in these areas where there was such spiritual decline that it seemed the devil was trying to get the victory there. He didn't, but we did a lot of warfare praying, which we had not had to do before to that extent. And the whole mission had just really disintegrated .... the snakes were all over, there was no water ... the women would have to go to the spring where the water was just oozing out of the ground."

This spring was about a mile or so from the station, and during this dry season, lining up to get water had become a round-the-clock job for the women. "They would stand in line all night waiting for the water to ooze back up, because it came so slowly," Geneva said.

Mrs. Fiakona, affectionately called 'Mollie' by those who knew her best, had been in such a line during this trip to the spring. She had had to wait overnight for water.

"When morning came, she was the next to step down, and another lady stepped in front of her and took her place. She was so angry, but being the pastor's wife, she didn't dare explode right there. She took her pot and went home, without water, and Fiakona said to her, 'What's the matter, mamma?'

'Another woman took my place in the line, and I don't have a bit of water to make breakfast or anything.'

"He said, 'Quit fussing about that. God is still in heaven. He is going to send us rain. It's just going to be for us, because you did what you could, now God is going to send us rain.'

"And she looked at him as if he had lost his marbles. But he was an unusual man of faith.

"He said, 'Put the big basins out around the house underneath the eaves, and God will send rain.' At Wasolo, it doesn't rain at all during the dry season, unless it is a very unusual circumstance. And on this day, the sky wasn't even cloudy!

"But after a while, the clouds came up, and it just poured over their place. There was an abundance of water for those at the top of Wasolo Hill.

"After the rain, Fiakona went down to see the director of the hospital at the base of the hill, about three blocks away. He asked him, 'Did you get the rain today?' And he said, 'No way! Of course not.'

"And Fiakona said, 'We did, but it was God's present to us. That was our rain.'

"He was unusual, to say the least," Geneva said, "and she didn't have to wait another night to get a pot of water."

Chapter 10

Disciplining Disciplers

The second term of their missionary career was the time of greatest focus and recognition of how Gordon and Geneva would be most effective as missionaries. One thing that became clear to them was that they would be spiritually reproducing themselves in Africa. The verses in II Timothy 2:1-2 became a foundation stone for their efforts:

> *Thou therefore, my son, be strong in the grace that is in Christ Jesus. And the things that thou hast heard of me among many witnesses, the same commit to faithful men, who shall be able to teach others also.*

This became their emphasis for the rest of their lives in Africa.

"There were times in the history of the Christian Church where there were no buildings, no organizations, but there were those discipling others," Gordon says. "That's why we heard the Gospel. So that principle of 'discipling disciplers' was crystallized during that revival and then throughout our ministry. And that's what Geneva was doing, reproducing herself in the lives of these women."

The second concept that became a foundation stone for their ministry: Trials do not make a person, they reveal a person.

"For anyone going on a foreign field, whether it is industrialized or primitive, the situation is the same," Gordon says. "There are loads of trials. And we conveyed this to the Africans, 'You are going out there, and some of you, in the providence of God, are going to lose children. And they are going to go to heaven. What you teach in that time through your example is of much more importance than what you preach from the pulpit.

"'There will be trials of all kinds. Financial problems. You'll reach the end of your resources financially. You will have people who will try to put curses on you. You'll have all of that. But in the midst of it all, the trials do not make you or break you, they simply reveal what Christ has worked into you. So the big thing is to work into yourself through the Word, and prayer, and every means available — work the Godly fabric into your life, so when the trials come, they will reveal what God has worked in you.'"

Geneva adds: "It is not a matter of if they come, it's when they come."

The third concept that became a foundation stone of their missionary work was the emphasis on sound marriages.

"If we don't have anything to say about the marriage of the African, we don't have anything to say, period," Gordon says. "That is the crux of the problem in Africa. How to take two people with sometimes totally divergent backgrounds, and have them live together, and sleep in one bed, and raise those kids, night and day being confronted with trial after trial — that is their problem. The problem is not theological. Africans have basically said, over and over again, 'We don't understand you white people. You are concerned about theological niceties. You are concerned about splitting hairs theologically. What we are concerned about is how to survive spiritually and how to get on with the task."

And that "how" is deeply embedded in the stewardship of marriages.

"Paul brings up in most of his writings the husband-wife relationship, and children," Geneva says. "I think what he stresses so much is that a marriage relationship is the picture to the whole world what Jesus Christ is to his bride. It makes marriage much more than just a human concept of two people coming together and making a home. Because in Paul's writings he makes it very clear that this is the way God has chosen to reveal to the world the love of the Lord Jesus Christ for his church. ... That is God's way of getting this picture to the world. The world can't understand spiritual concepts, but they can see them in people.

"We have learned and taught the Africans through the years that the husband is the representation of Christ in the home. The wife is the representation of the body of Christ, which is his church. And how you interact is teaching everybody just how Christ interacts with his church. As a consequence, they are learning by watching you. They are not learning principally by what you say. You can sketch the broad outlines in verbal communication, but you flesh it out with your life actions and your marital testimony."

The fourth foundation stone that was laid in that second term, that time of realization, was the rearing of children.

"We were of course in the thick of it while we were doing this teaching," Gordon says. "There were things we did right, certainly things we did wrong. But one of the things we did right was inculcate the Word of God into our children. Whenever we were at our table, morning and night, we would share the Word of God with them. ... We would take one verse a week and start to learn it bit by bit. By the end of the week, they could point to somebody and say, 'Okay Susan, what is I Thessalonians 5:17 and then the reference?' Then Susan, if she got it right, could call on someone else. This went on all through their growing years."

Geneva says it served the children well. When one of their children was at college and faced a very difficult situation, in a flash of realization the Lord brought to mind a Bible verse learned in that childhood game. The course of action suddenly became clear. "Scripture memorization I think is extremely important to build in children, and as adults, we have to keep at it."

"That's regarding children. Now when you view the old cultural African way of raising children, it is exactly contrary to this," Gordon says. "For example, if your child steals and repeatedly steals, the thing to do is chop off the finger or smash the fingernails. And what did that do? Engrain bitterness into that child. 'My dad chopped off my finger!'

"Then the end result was exactly the opposite of what they would really have liked to have seen. They would have liked to see good friendship, good fellowship. In the old African culture, the child was a tool, just like the woman. ... Of course, the Christian concept is exactly opposite. This child is not to be used, a child is someone you pour your life into. You are reproducing your Christian concepts and character and all, so if you disappear from this earthly scene tomorrow, your child can carry on."

"One of the difficulties," Geneva says, "is that they begin to learn the concept of loving their wives, loving their children, but they begin interpreting love as leniency. This has been a very hard thing for them to understand, that love does not mean leniency. But it means a discipline that is good for the child and not intended for you to vent your frustration.

"A verse that has been very meaningful is in Ephesians 6. It always amazes me that the Lord always has something to say about the situation we are trying to deal with:

> *Children, obey your parents in the Lord: for this is right. Honour thy father and mother; which is the first commandment with promise; That it may be well with thee, and thou mayest live long on the earth. And, ye fathers, provoke not your children to wrath; but bring them up in the nurture and admonition of the Lord.* — Eph. 6:1

"'Honor your father and mother' — you know parents love to read this. But then it says, 'Now a word to you parents.

Don't keep scolding and nagging your children, making them resentful, but bring them up in loving discipline. The Lord Himself approves of suggestions and Godly advice.'

"This is the thing — their way of discipline — that would make the child so upset and so angry and getting the roots of bitterness going down."

That bitterness would often erupt in the teen years, Geneva says, and later on when the parents were aged and turning to the children for support. It was not uncommon for adult children to settle old scores with parents, or neglect them, once the tables were turned and a parent was the dependent one.

"Another thing we tried to teach them is it is not a shame for the man to help his wife or his children," Geneva says. "That has been something demeaning for a man. He can see his wife coming down the road with a heavy load on her head — that's her responsibility. He sits and waits until she gets there.

"Through the years, we have tried to help them see that it is scriptural to help one another. At the Bible Institute, as these men were learning that, we would say, 'Hey, your women are going to be in school, you are going to have to help with this work.' And this was hard at first."

"Revolutionary," Gordon says.

"And when one of them started to do that, they had to really take a bold step, because the others laughed at them, made fun of them."

Geneva says getting the school away from the mission station and establishing its own grounds at Goyongo was a big help.

"There we were as one community with all students," she says. "When a wife gave birth, they didn't have a string of relatives to come and do the work. The other women would help as they could, but they had their families. The husband had to take care of these other children. He had to help her.

And this was very good for their wife-husband relationship to be helping one another. Some might say, 'There you were wrecking their culture.' No, we weren't wrecking their culture. It helped build relationships that have stood them in good stead as they get out in the work. ... And you can even find men now, pastors, who will come with a bucket of water on their heads. Or even a log on their heads carrying home for firewood. Helping their wives because they are coming behind with a full load, too.

"Through this, wives have developed a new respect for them. And the children are developing a respect for them. Because when you are worked to the bone and see that husband just sitting in a chair — maybe he's been out doing his thing, visitation if he is a pastor — but he doesn't lift his hand to the work, inwardly the women would begrudge him a lot.

"I know, because I've sat with them while they're pounding their corn, and they see their husband coming down the road, and you can't imagine the kinds of things they say about him. Then the little children learn this too, that worthless daddy is coming home, and we're going to have to feed him and get him his bath water while we go down to the river to bathe.

"We told the father, 'You have to earn the right to do the kind of discipline and so forth you want to do for your children. You have to earn the right to have the voice you want to wield around here. And part of that is earned by applying yourself to the family situation and helping.'"

"Another thread that has gone through our entire ministry is one of cooperation, unity, fellowship and love," Gordon says. "The old African culture was based on the poison cup, the hex, the witch doctor, and even within the family, the husband pointing out the wife as the cause of the death of a child. Or going to the witch doctor, who might say, 'It is the mother-in-law who has done it this time.' Can you imagine going to the mother-in-law and telling her, 'You are the reason my child has died?'

"The devil had built into the African culture sure failure for the family. Absolutely no way could that family succeed, the way the African culture is built around the demonic and the whole lifestyle of the people. Then, here comes a person who is converted. And we say, 'Hallelujah, he's converted.' What most of the church leaders don't realize is that this person has brought all this baggage. So church members who are newer Christians will accuse each other of going to the witch doctor, or of putting a hex on them. So a thread of our whole ministry has been to say, 'The old is gone. The new has come.' If any man be in Christ — and Paul wasn't talking to the unconverted when he said that; he was talking to converted Corinthians. He said, 'If any man be in Christ, he is a new creation. The old things are past and the new has come.' The problem with the Corinthians was there was too much of the old. And the challenge we have thrown out to the African church is, 'Your relationships are primary.' Jesus said, 'By this all men shall know that you are my disciples, not by your preaching, not by your all-night vigils, not by your Big Sundays or celebrations. It will be by your love.'"

Another thread: the need for periodic revivals. Without it, churches go into doldrums. Gordon says that is the problem in the U.S. church today. "Any group, you name it, was born in revival," Gordon says. "The Nazarenes, the Assembly of God, Christian Missionary Alliance. The same is true of the Covenant Church.

"There are periodic revivals that keep the springs open. Without the unclogging of the springs, there is sure calcification. Then all the people start talking about is what kind of music are we going to have in the church. ... When there is revival, the hearts of people are unclogged, and they say, 'It doesn't matter. If this speaks to that group of people, I'm for it.'"

The Christensens in 1961: From left, Michael, Gordon, Mary Lynn, Geneva and Susan.

CHAPTER 11

A NATION IN TURMOIL

There was no way Gordon and Geneva could have known at the beginning of their third term in 1958 that they would be ministering in the Belgian Congo at the pivotal point of its history. But the nation that would become Zaire burst onto the international stage in 1960, riveting the attention of Cold War enemies Dwight Eisenhower and Nikita Kruschev from their vantage points in the White House and Kremlin. Resource-rich Congo was becoming an independent nation, and both superpowers wanted it to align with them.

The Belgian Congo joined other European colonies in calling for independence. The winds of freedom had long been blowing by 1957, when the Gold Coast, a British colony, peacefully concluded years of preparation and became the nation of Ghana. Likewise, France began relinquishing control to its colonies as it realized it would have to fight nationalist forces to keep them. Before doing so, it had educated a generation of intellectuals, and in 1958 offered its colonies the option of independence in association with France or freedom and *au revoir* to its colonial masters.

Belgium, however, had misjudged the mood in the Belgian Congo and had not prepared for its independence. It had not prepared any of the Congolese for national leadership. It had ignored higher education and left elementary education for the most part to missionaries. It concentrated on using the Congolese as aides and clerks for Belgian overseers. The Belgians saw the Congolese as children and had no plans to grant freedom.

Nevertheless, they considered the Belgian Congo a model colony of peaceful, contented Africans. They didn't recognize the resentment that had festered in the people who had suffered years of cruelty and derogatory treatment.

Belgium had controlled the Belgian Congo since the late 1800s, when European leaders split Africa among themselves and recognized much of the Congo as the personal property of King Leopold. His exploitation of its abundant rubber and ivory made him fantastically rich, but he gathered his treasure with such cruelty that it became an international scandal. As a result, Leopold was forced in 1908 to turn over control to the Belgian government. A newly established Colonial Ministry eliminated the harshest abuses and teamed with giant mining interests to tap the rich stores of gems and metals in the Belgian Congo, particularly Katanga, a province in the southeast. By 1960, the Belgian Congo supplied 75 percent of the world's industrial diamonds and was a leading supplier of cobalt, tin, copper and gold as well as a mineral of special interest to the superpowers — uranium.

Yet the Belgians were caught off guard in 1959 when riots erupted in Leopoldville, leaving at least 42 dead. The Congolese were chanting "White man, go home" and demanding immediate independence. The Belgians in 1957 had initiated some very modest experiments in self-government with elections of African "mayors" for different parts of Leopoldville. But with violence erupting, Belgium began the hastiest of departures from Africa. In 1959 Belgium's King Baudouin quelled the Leopoldville riot (one of several) with a promise of independence. In January 1960 the Belgian government met with the leaders of the dozens of political parties that had suddenly mushroomed in the Belgian Congo. After a few weeks of tough negotiations, Belgium declared that a national election for African leaders would be held in three months, and the Belgians would relinquish control in six months to the new Republic of the Congo.

Any hope of a peaceful transition was shattered shortly after Independence Day, June 30, 1960. The new prime minister, Patrice Lumumba, saw the independence celebrations degenerate into tribe-based rioting. On July 5, his army mutinied against the Belgian officers who were supposed to be ushering in a transition but had not promoted one African to officer. The military soon turned its anger on all Europeans, causing race-based violence and a rush of frantic Belgian citizens trying to get out of the country.

Four days later, Belgium announced it was sending troops into the Congo to protect the whites there. With the despised colonial suppressors now taking on the role of foreign invader, the mayhem spread. Lumumba turned to the United Nations to help him restore order with U.N. troops and to keep the Belgians out.

Amid all this chaos, resource-rich Katanga announced July 11 that it was seceding from the new republic. Prime Minister Lumumba accused the Belgian mining interests of masterminding the plot to protect their holdings.

The chaos in the Congo dominated the world stage, with different scenes played out at the United Nations, Washington, Moscow and capitals across Africa and Europe.

Kruschev saw a golden door into Africa through the Congo and had already been trying to win favor there with promises of financial and military aid. Eisenhower saw another possible Cuba, with Lumumba another possible Castro — a view that Lumumba did not help with angry anti-European speeches. Dag Hammarskjold, secretary-general of the United Nations, reportedly said the Congo was "one of the most disheartening messes he had ever encountered."*

Gordon and Geneva had seen the beginnings of all this unrest when they returned to Africa in 1958 to begin their third term as missionaries.

They had spent July 1957 to August 1958 on leave in the United States, visiting churches coast to coast while the kids spent time with family in Kansas. Gordon was taking classes at Bethany College in Lindsborg, Kan., to get a B.A. in education and a teacher's certificate, keys to re-entering the Belgian Congo with the professional classification of schoolteacher instead of pastor. Little Susan also was in school, starting first grade in Lindsborg, while 3-year-old Michael learned a lot at home, particularly about an exciting new substance that fascinated him — snow. He delighted in making tracks with the tricycle his Grandpa and Grandma Noren gave him.

Susan also had some lessons to learn about this winter season that she had never before experienced. When, one day, she saw a beautiful icicle on her way home and decided to make it a gift for her mother, Susan was shocked to get home and find it missing from her pocket, which was now very soggy. This was a new world for the Christensen children.

---

*From a State Department cable sent by the U.S. Embassy in Leopoldville Aug. 5, 1960.

It also was the time of an addition to the family. During this leave, Gordon and Geneva's third child, Mary Lynn, was born.

In August 1958, with independence still two years away, the family returned to the Belgian Congo by airline, traveling from Chicago, New York, Lisbon to Leopoldville and then to Libenge, a city in the Ubangi region.

The Bible Institute was still trying to get established at its new site, Goyongo. When Gordon, Geneva and their children arrived, there were two small cottages made of locally sawed boards for missionary housing, and 40 student families were housed in the familiar mud houses they had built. Two long classrooms of mud and thatch completed the new jungle "campus."

Goyongo was actually more jungle than campus in 1958. The site was actually dank and dark then, still overshadowed by mammoth trees that surrounded it. They were so large that sunlight barely penetrated the foliage even at midday. This presented serious health problems for everyone.

"This was a hard time for us as a family," Geneva says. "Susan, at age 7, went away to boarding school at Karawa. This truck trip took five to eight hours, depending on the roads. Also, Gordon was gone much of the time, even though teaching, because we realized the church needed to have a well defined constitution and Africans must be in leadership. Independence was now uppermost in their minds."

The preparations in the wake of the pending break between Congo and Belgium, and the uncertainty of what that would do to missionary efforts, meant a lot of trips and countless hours working with African leaders of the Covenant and the Free Church, which was operating under the same charter as the Covenant.

"By early 1960, we faced a lot of uncertainty," Geneva says. "There were rumors of all kinds. June 30th became the target date for independence. We were praying that the unrest in lower Congo wouldn't reach us. However, we had some 'scram bags' ready."

The remote Goyongo campus, as well as Bokada station, which was about 38 miles from the campus, were the closest church sites to the border of the neighboring country, the Central African Republic, on the other side of Ubangi River. The Bible Institute was not yet hooked up to the missionary inter-station radio system, so at first it was largely uninformed of any evacuation plans or news of the unrest brewing down country. To the Christensens, there seemed to be no serious threat.

It wasn't long after Independence Day, June 30, and the ensuing riots that the local Belgian administrator came to the Bible Institute and told the Christensens and Free Church members that they had to leave for their own safety. Several caravans of people, mostly Belgian and Portuguese traders, had already passed through in the night on their way to the border, and then Covenant and Free Church missionaries from stations farther in came through in truck caravans.

The Christensens, along with two other families from the Free Church and two single women, headed for Bangui a couple days later. It was a four- to six-hour drive over rutted roads and lashed-log bridges to the Ubangi River. They arrived in the dark of night at Zongo, which is across the river from the city of Bangui, and loaded the trucks onto a ferry. Once safe on the other side, they were taken to a Brethren school compound, where they found the other missionaries "established" in its open-air classrooms.

"Each family staked out their area by blocking it in with trunks," Geneva says. "The buildings just had cement block walls chest high and tin roofs. We staked out our quarters and got our five camp cots set up. All of us ate together, we washed clothes in buckets and camped for a week. We were then told by the American Embassy that we would not be able to return to Congo, so a big Globe Master plane that had flown in food to the lower Congo from the U.S. was coming to fly us out."

However, Gordon and other missionaries realized that the church in Congo wasn't ready for everyone to leave. Some briefly returned to Congo to talk with the African church leaders, and then the missionaries as a group decided that the women and children should fly out on the military plane, and the men stay to help the Congolese church until they personally felt it was time to get out. They thought that would be a few days, maybe weeks.

Upon hearing of the plan, officials of the American Embassy warned that the men were going back at their own peril; it would take no responsibility for people returning to Congo.

"About mid-July 1960, we all piled into the trucks and headed for the airport, where the Globe Master had arrived the night before," Geneva says.

The plane was a giant prop transport, with a nose that could swing open to load trucks or heavy equipment. Inside, the plane had two levels, and bucket seats lined the sides. There was no bathroom: "They graciously put a canvas around a couple of garbage cans for that purpose," Geneva says.

The group took off in the giant plane with no knowledge of its destination. The military craft headed north.

"Flying over the Sahara Desert in the heat of the day in an unpressurized cabin was disastrous," Geneva says. "We were all lying on the floor, sick. While we ate, they pressurized the cabin."

The plane landed at a U.S. military installation in North Africa, where the missionaries received a meal before the plane took off — with a pressurized cabin — for a flight over the Alps. The next day, the group was in Frankfurt, Germany.

"After two weeks or more in Germany, we Covenanters were sent to Sweden to a couple summer camps for housing," Geneva says. "We also met up with some of our other missionaries who had evacuated from the northeast corner of our field, Wasolo. My sister-in-law Ruth Noren and her children were in that group.

"Each day we waited for news that we could return, but that never happened. Some of the women and children started leaving in August for the U.S. to get located and get children ready for school. I left with our children Labor Day weekend. My folks had found a small, furnished house just across from the grade school in Oberlin, my hometown."

The trip home without Gordon wasn't easy, not only because of the difficult trip, but also because of the heartache of leaving him behind in such uncertainty.

"Traveling with the three children, a big suitcase and other bags was a challenge," Geneva says. "Mary Lynn was just 2 years old and needed carrying a lot. Michael, who was 5, and Susan, 9, managed the handbags while I juggled tickets and Mary Lynn. We had a rough trip across the Atlantic in a four-motor prop plane. We came into New York late, and our connecting flight was gone. I will always be thankful to a floorwalker who picked up a phone and asked them to hold a plane so we could get on.

"My parents were relieved to hear my voice on the phone from Chicago that night. We went by train the next day to McCook, Neb., where the folks were waiting to take us to our temporary home in Oberlin. I kept things partially packed, ready to go back at a moment's notice. Our hearts were in Congo."

The bags would stay packed for months longer than the Christensens first imagined — almost a year — while political turmoil and violence shook the newly formed Republic of Congo.

Fortunately for Gordon, The Bible Institute was too remote to be directly affected by the upheaval in the early days, though it was only a matter of time before the storm would reach Goyongo as well.

Gordon, as well as Norman Barram, resumed work on what was becoming a very effective Bible Institute curriculum, while fellow missionary Jack Dangers concentrated on the construction of new classrooms and housing for African instructors. In addition to work on the site, the men went out into the surrounding area to teach Sunday school classes and evangelize.

However, home and family were always on their minds. The one distraction they had was their work.

Truck trips to the port city of Bangui to receive and send mail were weekly occurances, Gordon says. "It never seemed a chore to pile into the Goyongo truck and take off for Bangui. One or two letters would keep us going emotionally.

"Christmas came, but we were almost under oath to one another to not even mention what former Christmases were like or what our families might be doing during the holidays. One African, Karawa Adolph, a student at Goyongo, gave us each a tiny present, duly wrapped. Aside from that, there were no festivities."

In Kansas, Geneva and the children had been living almost day to day, waiting for a call to return to Congo. But the school year had begun, the children had enrolled in classes and Geneva had begun quite an itinerary of speaking engagements at churches. Day after day, the bags sat ready for a phone call that never came, and life insisted on moving forward.

"My parents were wonderful in trying to fill the void of Gordon's absence," Geneva says. "On weekends they would pick us up and take us out to the farm. Dad pulled the kids around the farm in a little red wagon he had bought for them.

"Susan did well at school, but Congo was her home. Michael found it like a prison to wear a shirt and shoes and have to sit at a desk. He was starting first grade. Mary Lynn, at 2 years, was looking for her daddy. She just couldn't understand all the change. Our first Sunday at church, she stood up, pointed a finger at the preacher and said, 'There's my daddy!'"

While Geneva saw a lot of hardship at this time, she also received a spiritual breakthrough she had needed. She had reached a point where she felt she had stopped growing. It had been a personal concern on top of all the family turmoil.

"I did quite a lot of speaking in churches and other organizations during that time. It was a real opportunity to witness. This is a period when the Psalms really spoke to me, and yes, I was beginning to grow in faith again. The daily need to totally rely on God for Gordon's well-being as well as guidance for helping the children through their difficult time broke me out of the no-growth period."

In December the Missions Office informed Geneva that her family, as well as the family of fellow missionary Ruth Ann Peterson, could return to the field after Christmas.

"I was elated, and so were the children," Geneva says. "We had to get new passports and were ready. My folks took us to McCook once again to board the train for Chicago. We arrived in Chicago in a blizzard. I left the kids with the baggage and went looking for a taxi. When we pulled up in front of the mission house, Harvey and Ruth Widman poked their heads out of their apartment window and said, 'You might as well go back; the way is closed to go back to Congo.'

"My heart sank. The kids were sick all night because of shattered hopes — they had been just two days from seeing their daddy.

"We took the next train back to McCook and got installed in the little house again. This time I unpacked, bought a car and tried to have a more stable home for all of us. Now I asked Gordon to make plans to return to us after the school year instead of us trying to go out there."

The next five months went better for all of them in Kansas. They started checking off the months until Gordon would be back, then the weeks, and finally days.

A Nation in Turmoil

In Congo, the political upheaval was worsening as months passed. The United Nations sent forces to help restore order.

"In our area, the Nigerians were the first to arrive," Gordon says. "Some slept in front of our house. It was unnerving to hear them talk about the grenades strapped to their uniforms."

"The next to arrive was a contingent of Egyptian soldiers under the command of a Capt. Hassan. They were even more dangerous, because they had only a smattering of knowledge of English."

This danger became most apparent to Gordon during one of the weekly mail trips to Bangui. Gordon and Jack Dangers arrived late and decided to spend the night in a tiny motel there. There was a curfew in effect, but during the night Gordon developed a terrible headache, one so bad that he decided to risk a few steps outside to get some aspirin he had in the door pocket of the truck.

"The door creaked and groaned when I opened it, and immediately an Egyptian guard called to me in Arabic," he says.

The situation turned into mayhem. The guard, then his partner, started screaming at Gordon in Arabic. Gordon had no idea what they were saying, but he apparently wasn't doing what they wanted, because they just screamed louder. Then Gordon heard and understood the universal message of a rifle cocking to fire. He was in deep trouble.

"I knew he wouldn't understand me in English, so I yelled out the name, 'Captain Hassan!' over and over, and walked toward him and his fellow soldier. They finally understood through sign language that I had a headache and had to go to the truck for aspirin."

Gordon's relations with Egyptian forces improved slightly after that, however, when they drafted him into service as an interpreter.

"The interpretation was generally from English to Lingala," Gordon says. "Egypt having been a part of the British

Empire, they knew English as a second language. But, of course, the villagers needed a Lingala translation.

"Being interpreter for the Egyptian force was not a real good situation, since it didn't appear to me they were appreciated by the populace in general. The unrest, separation from family, and the sight of guns all around us made for a lot of uneasy nights for me."

Gordon carried on at Goyongo as well as serving as an interpreter for the Egyptians into May 1961, when he and the others at Goyongo agreed he should head for home after the institute's graduation exercises.

"Those last five months we didn't have regular mail," Geneva says. "Sometimes we went without for quite some time. Another testing of my faith.

"Then we got word that Gordon would be home for Susan's 10th birthday on May 29th! I scrubbed and waxed all the floors, and we were all awaiting the call from Chicago saying he'd arrived.

"Finally a call came, but it wasn't Gordon. Ken Lundell from the Missions office said Gordon's plane had trouble and went back to Paris. Hopefully he would be in tomorrow."

"Trouble" was an understatement. After a family upheaval that was supposed to last just a few days had turned into a 10-month separation, and Gordon had nearly been shot by a U.N. soldier, his trip home nearly ended in disaster — twice.

"As the time for graduation approached, I wrote to Geneva, asking her to give me some advice on when to return to the United States," Gordon says. "I could either hurriedly wrap things up and take the quickest plane to the states or spend some time doing things in a more relaxed and orderly fashion. Geneva opted for the latter, which made a difference of flight departure time of just two weeks. If I had gone in the 'grab bags and run' mode, I would have gone down on the Bangui-to-Paris flight that crashed on a mountainside in

Africa. I am ever grateful to God for a wife who waited upon God for her directions and advice."

The flight Gordon did catch, however, had "trouble" that Geneva only knew vaguely about at the time. Gordon's jet from Belgium to Chicago had an engine 'flameout' over the English Channel and started a rapid dive for the sea.

"Never did Disney World in their wildest imaginations dream of such a ride!" Gordon says. "It was a mad descent. Around 1,500 feet above the Channel, the engines finally started and we limped back to Brussels. All the while, Geneva knew nothing except that we had 'technical difficulties.' Thank God for the train ride that brought me to McCook and a reunion with my family. Indescribable emotions of relief and joy welled up within me as I caught sight of Geneva, Susan, Michael and Mary Lynn on the train platform with Dad Noren."

"The older children quickly made friends again," Geneva says, "but Mary Lynn went and got Gordon's picture and said, 'That's my daddy.' Finally she consented to go alone with him for an ice cream cone, and that did it. Now he was her daddy, too."

It was a great summer of reaffirming family ties and getting over the year. But the recuperation was for the summer only. Word came shortly after Gordon's arrival in Kansas that the Christensens were needed back in Congo in August because there was no one to take their place at the Bible Institute for the next year. So Gordon and Geneva spent some time assisting at church summer camps on the West Coast and visited Gordon's family before heading back to the field.

It was good to be back on the field as a family from the fall of 1961 to the summer of 1962. Gordon and Geneva taught at the Bible Institute at Goyongo. Susan and Michael were able to go to the boarding school at Karawa, since several missionary families had returned. Mary Lynn and her friends had plenty of room to run, play and pick flowers on the hillsides of Goyongo.

"We would like to have thought that things were getting more normal, but soldiers, roadblocks and a totally confused people, trying to figure out what 'independence' was, made for some tense moments during the year," Gordon says.

In the summer of 1962, they left for a much-needed furlough, especially on Gordon's part.

"We moved into Geneva's Grandmother Carlson's house in Oberlin," he says. "She went to live with a daughter, as she wasn't well. Before leaving, she made sure every doilie was in place."

Susan and Michael were able to be in the same school they had been in when the family evacuated in '60-'61. That was helpful, Gordon says. Mary Lynn kept busy with her dolls, collecting lady bugs and playing with a little neighbor. Gordon was on the itineration schedule.

"It was a good year," he says.

LIFE LESSONS

The unexpected 10-month separation made Gordon and Geneva re-evaluate priorities and make some new family vows.

"I determined that I would not leave my family for such a protracted period again if the circumstances would indicate an evacuation," Gordon says. "This is, in fact, the procedure we followed from that point on: my wife first, my family second, and ministry third. It became my motto for work and life after this first evacuation."

Gordon also said he learned a lesson about not becoming so riveted by news that you come to a standstill as big events swirl around you. "We needed to quit listening to all the news on the radio and start making some news through 'warfare praying,' or make-a-difference prayers," he says.

Geneva says that the evacuation reinforced for her the fact that God can give peace even when there are no outward appearances that a situation is improving.

"God is faithful," she says. "He goes before and prepares the way. And God uses difficult circumstances to grow our faith."

Chapter 12

Deeper Into Chaos

The Christensens returned to Africa on a beautiful new freighter to begin their fourth term. The trip was the closest thing to luxury they would know for a year, for they were steaming into a civil war.

Instantly they could sense the tension when they arrived in the port city of Matadi in the fall of 1963. The political and social chaos that had begun with independence was continuing, with superpowers in the background supporting different sides.

In the summer of 1963, rebel attacks had begun with the sabotage of government buildings, bridges and ferries. The rebels were linked to Communist China; one of the principle organizers, Pierre Mulele, had spent one-and-a-half years in exile in Egypt and Communist China before returning to Africa. He and other deposed political leaders of the Belgian Congo were the hub of the National Committee of Liberation, which claimed Congo needed to be freed from foreign control, and had the clear support of Communist China. But anti-"European" (meaning caucasian) sentiment had been running high among all the people of Congo, even as their top leaders and opponents scrambled to get aid from Western, U.N., or Communist sources. When Gordon, Geneva and their three children landed in Matadi, they found not only a general uncertainty caused by an unstable government, but they were personally viewed with suspicion because they were white foreigners.

From Matadi they set out for Leopoldville, driving a mission pickup truck loaded with supplies. Before they were allowed to leave, they had to pay customs fees so high that they left the city almost penniless. They set out about 4 p.m., and by the time they had reached Thysville 127 miles away, Gordon had spent almost all the remaining money on gasoline. There was not even money for food for the children.

The Christensens pushed on through the pitch black night for Leopoldville. A heavy rain began as they drove down the paved road toward the nation's capital. Military checkpoints had been set up along the way in a government attempt to intercept any rebels trying to get into Leopoldville. Tensions were high.

Driving in heavy night rain, and with his family both tired and hungry, Gordon passed what looked like an unmanned checkpoint. When he heard the shriek of a guard's whistle, he knew he was wrong. He hit the brakes and slid to a stop, then backed up to the checkpoint and rolled down his window.

The guard was furious — and drunk or on drugs. He poked his rifle into the cab at Gordon.

"How would you like it if I shot you?" he yelled in Lingala. Then he jerked the door open. "You come with me!"

The soldier kept the rifle trained on him as Gordon stepped into the rain. Then the soldier marched him off to the front of the building, where he had a fire going.

Susan and Michael, who had been riding in the back of the truck, clambered to the window on the driver's side.

"What's happening to Daddy?" they asked Geneva.

"Don't you look!" Geneva responded. "You pray!"

Pray they did; very forcefully, Geneva recalls, and all the time she was listening for the rifle to go off.

While she fought to pray, her mind was assaulted with questions like, "What are you going to do with the body? Do you go and retrieve it? Flee in an effort to protect the children? What are you going to do?"

The moments dragged by. All was silent, except for the rain. Then Gordon and the soldier appeared out of the darkness.

The guard kept Gordon standing at the side of the truck while he badgered him with angry questions. Then it dawned on him and Geneva what was happening: this soldier was trying to get a bribe out of Gordon to let the family go on.

Finally the soldier told Gordon he needed to check the truck's lights. Gordon reached in the cab and flipped the turn signal. The yellow light began to flash methodically on the fender beside the soldier and quickly showed Gordon how drunk this man was. The blinking light seemed to break his addled line of thinking and almost put him in a trance. He lowered his rifle and looked at the light for a long time with bloodshot eyes. Then he turned away from Gordon and walked around the front of the truck, leaving Gordon standing in the rain, his foot on the running board. The interrogation apparently was over.

But the soldier came to Geneva's window, still hoping for a payoff.

For years, the mission policy was never to make a payoff, because it would unleash an unending cycle of blackmail. But as this soldier started ranting at Geneva, she responded by saying in Lingala, "You can have all the money in my purse."

That changed his tune, until he saw that there was very little money there, only a few small coins, and got insulted.

Then Geneva, stressed to the breaking point, let him have it with some Kansas plain talk, translated into Lingala: "Sure! That's what's happened to the country here. They've already taken everything we had! I couldn't buy bread for the kids back in Thysville!"

He backed up. He looked over the truck for another second, then waved them on.

They had already had a brush with disaster, and they hadn't even reached the Bible Institute yet. It was a glimpse of what the fourth term would hold: soldiers, guns, violence and death.

Further down the road, later into what was a very long, hard night and closer to the nation's capital, another whistle blew at another checkpoint. This time a group of soldiers started milling around the truck, looking for rebels that might be trying to get into Leopoldville. Geneva and the children were crowded into the cab now as a soldier stepped up to the driver's window and asked Gordon if there was anyone riding in the back.

"No," Gordon answered, "we're a missionary family traveling alone."

Then, through the rain, Gordon and the soldier both heard the sound of voices coming from the back of the truck!

"Then what is that sound!" the soldier bellowed. Gordon was in shock. What *was* that sound? He could almost feel the other soldiers tensing, getting ready for any surprises.

In an instant of recognition, Gordon understood. Packed in the truck bed was a portable radio. Jostling on the road must have turned it on. But the way the soldier had just asked the key question, and Gordon had just heard the sickening, contradicting sound at the same time he did, and with even the volume just right to be momentarily mistaken for whispers — Gordon couldn't have been set up any better to look like a liar.

He had to be quick, and he was. "That's a radio, and you're free to unload the truck and inspect it if you don't believe me," he said.

Perfect. The soldiers no more wanted to empty a truck on a dark, rainy night than the Christensens wanted to be driving in it. The pause was long enough for the voice to be recognizable as a radio announcement, and the tension eased. After a few more questions and a simple lookover of the truck, the soldiers let the Christensens move on.

About 10:30 p.m., the family reached the mission house in Leopoldville. The house was full with missionaries moving on or off the field amid the turmoil. The missionaries did find lodging for the Christensens: Geneva and the girls stayed in the apartment of fellow Covenant missionary Leola Johnson, and Gordon and Michael with the missionary family of Ken Wicklunds, all stationed in Leopoldville.

The other missionaries started cluing in Gordon and Geneva on what had been transpiring in the new Republic of Congo:

Rebel troops had been moving across the countryside in a murderous, and often drug-charged frenzy to "free" the just-freed nation from its current regime, still led by Patrice Lumumba. Based in East Congo, these soldiers would go on forays to kill government leaders and white foreigners. The anti-government message was spreading village to village and tribe to tribe, quickly moving toward Leopoldville and the western coast.

The forays were often led by children armed with rifles. Usually drugged with what was thought to be tea the Chinese had loaded with marijuana, these kids usually believed they were invincible. Coming behind in truck convoys would be adult rebel troops. Often the foray was overseen not by a military commander, but by a tribal witch doctor.

The target was anything that smacked of capitalism or the West: people who wore watches or imported shirts, for example. Of course, the witch doctors insisted, the white Christian missionaries were high on the list.

The Christensens spent several days in Leopoldville waiting for passage to go upcountry to the Karawa Mission, far north from the rebel target of Leopoldville. Geneva and the girls got a plane to Gemena while Gordon and Michael followed by another plane to Mbandaka, then by Disciples Missions plane to Gemena.

The Mission had a clearly defined mission statement for this time, to continue the work of evangelizing and delivering the Gospel to the African people. However, the overarching dread that the nation was about to collapse into full-blown war made it tough to stay focused on the goal. There were contingency plans to make so the missions and Bible Institute could operate in war conditions. Plans for supply routes were needed so food and medicines would get through in hard times.

The administrative needs of those tense times were enough to take everyone's complete attention so unrelentingly that the stated goal — evangelization and delivering the Gospel — could not only end up on the back burner, it could get pushed off the stove altogether.

But the unceasing administrative pressure was only part of the story. Gordon and Geneva were again dogged by sickness as well. Gordon came down with hepatitis, and the resulting diet he was put on then caused a stomach ulcer to flare up. He was mostly confined to his bed or the house for several months. Meanwhile, Geneva was taking care of him as well as working with the girls' school at Karawa and even serving as guest coordinator for the Karawa Station. Before long, she had contracted her third bout of hepatitis.

Across the country, rebel attacks continued against government forces and Christian missionaries.

In January 1964, President Joseph Kasavubu declared a state of emergency in Congo's western Kwilu Province. Neighboring provinces were already falling into rebel hands. As they did, most missions were burned. Reports came out of missionaries being killed: Irene Ferrel of Jerome, Indiana, was murdered with a poison arrow at the Mangunugu mission; three Catholic priests at the Kilembe mission were slain by rebels armed with knives, bows and arrows. One of the most harrowing atrocities was the murder of as many as 19 missionaries trying to escape a foray who were caught at a riverside. In a show of hatred, their bodies were thrown to the crocodiles.

Tales of heroism were emerging as well: The Christensens heard of a Catholic cardinal at Kisangani protecting the people inside his mission compound. Rebels repeatedly ordered him to send the people out, but his response was, "Over my dead body." The rebels never touched him.

He also was known to boldly push through rebel roadblocks to help people on the other side.

The Christensens were stationed at Karawa instead of the Bible Institute in Goyongo; Gordon and Geneva had requested to be stationed where the two older children would be in school. They felt the family needed to be together.

In September 1964, rebels attacked the mission hospital at Wasolo. Wasolo was quite a distance from Goyongo, and even farther from Karawa. Yet word came from the U.S. embassy in Bangui that all Americans would have to evacuate; rebels were too close, and there was too much risk that Westerners would be taken hostage or killed.

By this time, Gordon and Geneva had endured almost a year of debilitating sickness. The evacuation of Karawa put the entire caravan of missionaries at the Bible Institute at Goyongo, where they stayed overnight. However, after that day's trip, Geneva — now suffering with pneumonia as well as hepatitis — was so sick that she told Gordon that she couldn't make it to Bangui. She told Gordon he should take the children with the caravan the next morning and leave her there. She would rest there and follow later.

Gordon said no, and when the caravan pulled out the next morning, it left the Christensen family alone at the Bible Institute.

For a week they stayed at the quiet camp while Geneva endured fever and exhaustion. However, the first day her temperature dropped came word from the American Embassy in Bangui that it didn't like the Christensens remaining behind, and if they could not evacuate, it would send in a military helicopter to get them out.

Gordon and Geneva said that would not be necessary. A mission truck had returned the day before to get the Christensens as well as three women who were at the Bokada station.

It was a radio message from Dr. Paul Carlson at Wasolo that had convinced them they had to evacuate as quickly as possible. Gordon and Geneva had been in radio contact with Dr. Helen Berquist, Dr. Teddy Johnson and Melvina Benson at Bokada. Like the other doctors, Dr. Carlson had remained behind to care for medical patients. He had sent his wife and family to safety across the river to Bangassou, but as the doctor at the Wasolo hospital, he felt he needed to stay a little longer.

During that delay, rebel forces attacked the hospital. It was mid-September, 1964.

Dr. Carlson sent urgent radio messages to the other stations, including Goyongo: "If you can get out, go!"

It was a big risk to send the messages, because everything he did was eventually reported to the rebels. They decided this was proof that he was a "spy," and he was taken captive, while black hospital staffers were mistreated and one killed.

The tragic fate of Dr. Carlson would become international front-page news, the subject of a cover story in Life Magazine and ultimately a book by his widow. He would be whisked back to the eastern part of the nation where the rebels were strongest, and held for "trial" with other white captives. During those days of captivity, his calm witness to his fellow prisoners, even during mock public trials and possible executions, inspired those with him.

Many of those captives were Europeans, and Belgium finally dispatched commandos to rescue them. During a ground assault in which the captives were able to be freed, mainly because a rebel's machine gun jammed before he could mow them down, only one captive was killed — Paul Carlson.

But his last radio contacts with his colleagues shortly before capture had moved the remaining doctors and missionaries, a group of 10, out of harm's way.

It was nighttime when the Christensens left in the two-truck caravan for Bangui in pouring rain. That rain was the perfect cover for their escape, because the rebels believed it was a taboo to do anything in the rain. But as had often occurred before, the primitive road bogged them down. When they reached a wooden bridge in the jungle, one of the trucks broke through.

It was a tense, frightening time. But amid the tension, Dr. Teddy Johnson began to laugh. Then she started a silly, slap-happy dance in the rain. Her clowning soon had the other missionaries laughing, clowning and playing in the rain as well. The tension snapped.

When the missionaries went back to work on the truck, they freed it by prying it out with poles. They got across the bridge, and soaked and muddy, kept driving for Bangui. Several hours later, they were safe on the other side.

The battle raged behind them, ending up in the yard of the Banzyville Church. The firefight at that church between rebel and government forces was to be the turning point of the rebellion in the northern region. But the fighting continued for months as the rebels were pushed back and eventually overcome.

When the smoke cleared, the fiery prime minister, Patrice Lumumba, was dead. The nation's first president, Joseph Kasavubu, was deposed but still alive, retiring to his farm in the southern part of the country, and the government's top general, Mobutu Sese Seko, was in power, where he would remain for 32 years. And the Belgian Congo-turned Republic of Congo would have a new name: Zaire.

In the Central African Republic, the Christensens stayed at the Brethren mission at Bossongoa, about a half-day's journey from the capital city of Bangui. The mission needed assistance, and though both Gordon and Geneva were recuperating from hepatitis, they agreed to stay and help as best they could. Though it was nowhere in their original plan for the term, and though they were wracked with sickness, this unexpected turn would prove to be one of the most important times of their ministry in Africa.

The living conditions were the best they had had in Africa and excellent for Geneva's recuperation. The tension of the civil war was off, and all the family could relax a little, although they were at the radio for every Voice of America newscast.

The living quarters at Bossongoa were built of cement block with concrete floors, had plumbing with an indoor bathroom and stainless steel kitchen sinks — exceptional conditions to the Christensens. Susan, 12, and Michael, 9, went to a missionary school at Bata, while Mary Lynn, 6, stayed with Gordon and Geneva for homeschooling.

Although the children were away for several weeks at a time, Gordon says the 10 months of calm was nevertheless a family-building time for them all. He recalls driving down to a nearby river when the kids were on break and watching the hippos in the water.

On the station, Gordon taught high school students and led the college Sunday school class. He studied yet another African language — Sango — daily with the local pastor at Bossongoa because the local people spoke mostly Sango with some French thrown in. Gordon wanted to be able to communicate with the congregation and populace of Bossongoa, and that required knowledge of Sango.

In these months Gordon and Geneva also launched what would become a key part of their ministry, writing Christian literature for the African church.

They had grasped early in their first term the need for literature. Dick Anderson, who was also staying in the Central African Republic at the Bata station, strongly encouraged them to keep writing and find a publisher. "Publish or perish," he would tell them again and again.

So for about three hours a day, Gordon and Geneva would work in their six-room house at the mission station, pounding out words on a manual typewriter. In the 10 months they were there, they wrote their first book in Lingala, *The Work of the Workman*, which discussed the responsibilities of pastors, deacons, other church leaders and lay members.

They also worked on a series of tracts in Lingala that covered many of the problems they had seen in earlier terms: wife beating, polygamy, witchcraft and hexes, puberty rites, poison-cup trials and the false reliance on dreams for guidance.

The poison cup was especially dreaded among villagers. It was given to a person suspected of having a malevolent spirit. If the accused went into convulsions or died after drinking the cup, it was deemed proof that he or she had a bad spirit and was responsible for a death or deaths in the village. The Biblical revelation that the new believer has no part in the demonic liberated some believers from voluntarily participating in the drinking of the cup.

These first efforts would transform the thrust of the rest of their missionary careers. From that point on, for what would be about half their time in Africa, they would work extensively producing literature for the church.

Of particular interest were the needs of women, for whom little had been done. While recuperating, Geneva worked on a series of lessons she called "The Happy Home," which was mimeographed in booklet form. In the 1990s, those early writings, written while Gordon and Geneva were expatriots in the Central African Republic, were still being reprinted and used.

Publishing the material, however, also took some doing.

It was while they were back in the U.S. on leave that they found a typesetter who could prepare the book in Lingala, a language virtually unknown outside Zaire, and a printer who would print and bind the books.

Part of that help came from a second cousin of Geneva's, Elna Larson, who lived in Kansas. Elna was a member of

Geneva's home church, the Herndon Mission Covenant Church. Elna was very missions minded and keenly interested in helping Gordon and Geneva. In fact, Geneva said, Elna "gave her whole life to home missions work." She sold a set of antique milk-glass dishes and raised $100 for the printing of *The Work of the Workman*.

The book was printed at the Bata Mission in early spring 1965 and distributed when the Christensens returned to Zaire that summer.

The rebels had been pushed back enough by early 1965 that the U.S. Embassy was letting Americans back into the country. Gordon and Dick Anderson would make the 10-hour drive back to the Bible Institute at Goyongo for two-week stays on the grounds. Because the Brethren would not allow women to stay alone at the mission station, Geneva stayed at one of the other mission stations.

Gordon says that the time spent with Dick Anderson traveling back into Zaire was a great learning experience for him. "It would be hours together, then teaching, eating together," Gordon says. Gordon says Dick helped him mature and was a prayer-life mentor. He allowed Gordon to make mistakes and learn from them. Gordon described Dick's chapel services as "sparks from the anvil."

For Geneva, she found the 10 months a time of learning about the grace and provision of God. Perhaps these were the vital times for the lessons to be taught, because it was so easy to slip into despair then. But several miracles gave her the desire and fire to keep going as a missionary.

After first arriving in Bossongoa, Geneva soon realized that the mission station was a key stopping point for people, especially missionaries, traveling to Bangui, the capital, and the west coast of Africa. But she didn't realize they would often arrive about noon without food, and though Geneva would sometimes find herself with only the simplest amount to offer, she would feel the tug at her heart to help the travelers and have them stay in the Christensen home.

On one occasion, she found herself with two missionaries who had driven up just as the family was about to eat. Geneva had almost nothing in the kitchen. What she had, she easily could have eaten herself — some chicken that didn't amount to the meat on a cornish hen, and a small dab of vegetables that might have made one serving.

She felt there was only one thing to do. She put the food on the table and then quietly went back into the kitchen. Her plan was to not eat at all, because there wasn't enough.

Several minutes later she came back to the table, where Gordon, Mary Lynn, and the two guests were sitting. She was shocked by what she saw.

Everyone was enjoying a full plate of food — and there was still food in the dishes! The serving bowls were passed around for second servings. No one seemed to be giving it a second thought, unaware of the terrible shortage Geneva had faced minutes earlier. Nor were they aware of what she was seeing now. Conversation and laughter wafted over the table as the people nonchalantly helped themselves.

Geneva never saw how the food multiplied, but as the dishes went around the table, they simply did not run out. There were even leftovers when the meal was finished.

For years, Geneva never told the story to anyone. She was overwhelmed by what she had experienced and what it meant. That meal, she says, is one of the most important experiences of her life.

But there were others during those 10 months. Was God giving her reassurances and lessons during this time, special lessons for a woman who a few months earlier had been so sick that she advised her family to leave her behind to an approaching rebel attack?

This was also the year of the special Christmas, Geneva says. Susan and Michael were home from boarding school. It was Dec. 21, and the Christensens were getting ready for a picnic down by the river when a Land Rover pulled up to their house. Two men and a woman were traveling from the west coast to South Africa. The two men were members of the Peace Corps. One of the men was the child of a missionary couple in China, and it was a childhood that had left him very bitter.

The three wanted to spend the night in the mission chapel. But Gordon and Geneva invited them to the picnic and said they could spend the night with them.

That evening, the Christensens sang some Christmas carols, and Gordon told the Christmas story. They even had a Christmas tree — a dead tree they chopped down and decorated with some tricks Geneva learned in her Dust Bowl days. They wrapped bits of cotton on the tree to make it look snow-covered, and then added decorations made out of coffee can lids and construction paper. When they had finished, Gordon put a desk lamp under the tree. It was beautiful.

The children drew a Monopoly board, and the homemade game became the group's entertainment for the evening. That night, Gordon and Geneva set up their camp cots in the living room for the men and arranged a bed in the office for the woman.

That night, she and the girl entered a long, thoughtful talk. Geneva shared spiritual truths about Jesus Christ, the Bible, and even the point of Christmas. It was a scene reminiscent of her childhood, when her mother would find an opportunity to witness to the young people she welcomed into the family farmhouse. All the concepts seemed new to this girl, and she gave Geneva rapt attention.

The next morning after breakfast, the group lingered with the family for hours. Something had touched and was holding them there.

Finally they loaded up the Land Rover and headed out for Bangui. Gordon and Geneva never saw the people again, but months later they got a letter from South Africa.

It was from the son of the missionaries to China. He thanked the Christensens for their hospitality, and said spending the night with them had been very meaningful to them. It was the only Christmas they had.

Gordon and Geneva knew it had been been special in some way . They weren't sure how, but they knew that the Christmas visit had been arranged by God, part of some master plan that they could not perceive but were privileged to play a part in. Gordon and Geneva have never learned what fruit resulted from that encounter, but they trust that one day they will know the whole story, and that it will be a great one.

A third miracle occurred during their 10 months at the Brethren mission. Gordon and Dick made one trip back to Zaire and Geneva and Mary Lynn went to stay at a rented facility the evacuated missionaries had in Bangui. When Geneva arrived, however, the place was so crowded that she volunteered to do a job that would get her out of there: deliver a Peugeot truck upcountry to Bogila. It had been in Bangui for repairs.

Geneva and several Africans started out on the trip, eventually traveling up a remote mountain road. Suddenly the truck engine died. Geneva got it over to the side of the road, and she and the Africans started looking for a mechanical problem. But they were all so unfamiliar with Peugeots that they couldn't even pop the hood!

Geneva and the Africans joined hands in prayer. They were stuck miles from nowhere and needed help.

Moments later, a Jeep carrying two French engineers came careening down the mountain road. The French government had sent technicians and professionals to the country, its former colony, to assist with major public works projects, such as a nearby hydroelectric system at Boali Falls.

The men were going way too fast as they roared around the curb and past Geneva, the Africans and the truck. Geneva saw the shocked look on the men's faces as they flashed past them on what was not a heavily traveled road. Then in a blur and cloud of dust, they were out of sight, having rounded the next curve.

Geneva was stunned as the jungle silence closed in again on the road. It had happened so quickly, it was as if it had never occurred. It took a moment to sink in that she had just avoided a disaster, because a crash would have been unavoidable if both vehicles had been on the road at the same time. Very easily, both Jeep and truck could have gone off the road and down the mountain to join a number of other vehicles that hadn't made it.

She climbed back into the truck, thanking God for saving her life. She turned the key and the truck roared to life without hesitation. That confirmed for her the thought that had flashed through her mind: God had gotten her off the road in order to save her.

Thus, the 10 months was a great time of growth for the Christensens, in terms of family unity, personal coaching, launching their writing ministry and reaffirmations that God was with them. Gordon says it proved not to be a hiatus in their lives, but it was a pathway for their spiritual growth.

In July 1965, Gordon and Geneva got permission to return to the Bible Institute. They loaded up a mission truck and started back across the border with their children.

It was the rainy season. Goyongo, the Bible Institute station, was dark and soaked. Within days, hard work and the weather was draining Geneva. She was also heavily burdened with concern about her children. What should they do about schooling? The Ubangi Academy (UBAC) would not be operating that year.

Before long she was bedridden. The Christensens were still alone at the Bible Institute when Geneva's heartbeat became so feeble, her breathing so labored, that both she and Gordon thought she was dying. Gordon went to Bosobolo, a state post and also Catholic mission about 10 kilometers from Goyongo. There he got some Catholic nuns who were nurses to come and help.

Geneva roused out of unconsciousness one time to find herself hooked up to an IV and two Catholic sisters praying fervently with their rosaries. She smiled to herself and thought the scene was funny. God had to have a sense of humor to wake her up and show her two devout Catholic nuns praying the rosary over this Protestant missionary in a cabin in Africa.

The nuns had returned to Bosobolo, and several days later, Gordon was cleaning a classroom while Geneva rested in bed and Susan managed the home.

Suddenly, Geneva seemed to feel her strength draining out of her. She asked Susan to make her some tea. She could feel herself passing out.

"Go get Dad," was the last thing she said before she lapsed into unconsciousness.

Yet Geneva did not feel unconscious at all. She could feel her and her entire bed rising from the room. She sensed she was traveling to heaven, and a verse from Jude came to mind:

"He will present you faultless to the Father."

The idea thrilled her as it never had before. It was as if the full meaning of that promise had suddenly opened to her, and there was new depth, new greatness in it.

"I was lying on my bed," Geneva recalls, "and I was thinking, 'The Lord Jesus is going to present me faultless to the Father! Me!' I was so exhilarated, I could hardly believe it. But my bed stopped outside a wall."

The Lord did not come to greet her at that wall. Instead, the bed started to descend. Then she was suddenly aware of her family, standing distraught around her bed, and Gordon was standing over her, saying, "Don't give up! Don't give up!"

"I thought, 'What is he talking about? What is the matter?' I had just had a fantastic experience, I had just been up to the portals of heaven waiting for the Lord," Geneva recalls. "For a long time, this really helped me. It also removed the fear of death from me."

When she had been getting so weak, she had worried about dying that night and Gordon and the children having to deal with a dead body. There was no one else to help.

Then, Geneva says, another miracle happened.

That night, after this brush with death, young Paul Anderson appeared at their window.

"Where's the key to our house?" was his greeting.

"Paul!" Gordon cried. "What are you doing here?"

Paul, the teenage son of missionaries Dick and Alpha Anderson, had come with his parents when they decided to return to the Bible Institute earlier than planned to prepare for their re-entry to Congo from the Central African Republic. Alpha was a trained nurse, so Geneva got wonderful, constant care until they could reach Dr. Titus Johnson. Communication, even with shortwave radio, was still difficult.

To further complicate matters, lightning had damaged the radio at Goyongo. Finally a porter carried a message to Dr. Johnson that Geneva was ill. He traveled to Goyongo from Karawa and examined Geneva, ordering her back to the states for medication and recuperation.

The Christensens left Goyongo Aug. 11 to start the long trek, by truck and small plane, to Leopoldville. Gordon, Geneva and the children boarded a Pan Am flight to Chicago, where Geneva was immediately admitted to Swedish Covenant Hospital. She stayed there several days being treated for exhaustion before being allowed to go home to Oberlin, Kansas.

Geneva stayed on the farm with her family for several weeks while Gordon looked for a place to live in town. During those weeks, the children stayed with Geneva's brother

Willard's family so they could ride the school bus. The family lived in Oberlin for the next year.

Meanwhile, members of the missions board of the Evangelical Covenant Church of America were wondering if they should ask the Christensens to write off missions work for the rest of their lives.

Life Lessons

Gordon and Geneva watched the personal pressure of their first years in Africa turn into a societal pressure during this term. It seemed like much of the culture had openly turned against them and their message. And the pressure that put on them easily could have distracted them from the true purpose for which they were in Africa: to evangelize.

Specifically, their concerns were protecting the African Christians who would face the possible turmoil in their country. They spent much time preparing for an evacuation and figuring out how they would reach out to and assist the Zairian Christians from positions outside the country.

It was very good work. But they had to be about the foremost work: spreading the Gospel, whether or not there was thunder on the horizon.

Gordon and Geneva hear such thunder outside the Christian churches of America in the 1990s. Surprisingly, churches are finding themselves more at odds with the government and culture they live in.

"One problem is that Americans don't believe in absolutes," Gordon says. "We have people working two, three, four jobs each. Then the church needs help on a work day? Ha! Then the church gets bogged down in our high-technology society. You can see it in their eyes. The vibrancy that used to characterize Americans just doesn't seem to be in their eyes anymore."

That "bogged down" church sees itself overwhelmed with financial problems, apathy, defeatism. Outreach can fade into the background when survival seems to be at stake.

But outreach has to remain Job No. 1 for the church, because of Jesus' Great Commission. Whether clear skies or clouds, today is the day to be about the Great Commission, whether in Africa or a church's neighborhood.

The other life lesson Gordon and Geneva learned during this term, particularly Geneva, was the abounding grace of God.

The family had gone through many hardships, and God made it clear that He was aware of them all. Geneva said He even used miracles to teach her. God made it clear that He could step into their daily lives by doing it:

I can do all things through Christ which strengtheneth me ...

> My God shall supply all your need according to his riches in glory by Christ Jesus — Philippians 4:13, 19

Though hardships and sickness seemed to fill each day, God was evidently with them. Nevertheless, His presence did not also mean the absence of problems. The Lord seems to choose instead to join us in many of our storms rather than still them.

In Africa during 1964 and 1965, diseases continued to ravage, rebels continued to threaten, good men like Paul Carlson continued to die doing good work. None of those things, Gordon and Geneva learned, translate into defeat for God or God's people.

"This is a lesson we've learned all through our missionary experience," Gordon says. "There is always a lesson to be learned, however severe the trial. However tragic may seem the circumstances, we learned that God uses every, every experience."

Chapter 13

Good Country Air

When the Christensens returned to Kansas in 1965, Gordon found a nice, sunny, two-bedroom house in Oberlin for the family. With some items from Geneva's parents, some pieces from the second-hand store and a new sofa bed that would double as Michael's bed, they quickly established a comfortable home. The children started in the public schools: Susan in ninth grade, Michael in sixth and Mary Lynn in second. Meanwhile, the World Mission office let Gordon stay home and care for the family, a gift of time that he and Geneva greatly appreciated, because Geneva had to spend a lot of time resting.

The children were happy to be at their American "home," near their grandparents, near their home church and in the familiar surroundings with which they had become acquainted during other furloughs. Gordon did a little speaking at nearby churches only, and Geneva continued to recuperate, until she had the strength on her father's birthday, Nov. 11, to bake and decorate a cake for him. For Geneva, it was a big and satisfying accomplishment, and one that tired her out.

Nevertheless, the days weren't boring. Gordon and Geneva loved the time with Susan, Michael and Mary Lynn. "Our children really added spice to our lives as well as to the lives of our neighbors," Geneva says. "One day a lady called and asked why our little girl carried her books on her head as she came home from school! I said, 'Oh? Does she? I hadn't noticed.' Then I told her we had come home from Africa and that's the way they carried things there. We left Africa for a time, but the customs came with our kids."

Slowly, Geneva regained her strength. Thanksgiving, then Christmas came and went. Each day brought improvement, but it couldn't be hurried. Any attempt to rush would only mean a setback. Geneva was learning a new pace — God's pace — and seeing how it had differed from her own. She was also learning the miraculous way that, while it can appear slow in human terms, it proves to be much more efficient and productive than the rushed, strain-and-drain approach of the world seeking productivity. While she had all her life wanted to walk with the Lord, she was seeing now that often she had tried to do so at her own hurried pace. In these months, she feels, He was teaching her to recognize when she was right in step with Him and trust that it was the best way to cover the most ground for His kingdom.

"By January I was feeling much better and even did some speaking once in a while," Geneva says. "The getting-well process was slow, and I had to learn patience. The Lord was training my work-oriented mind to realize that resting in Him was the priority."

But in the early spring of 1966, a letter arrived for Gordon from a Covenant Church in Canada, Malmo Mission, 60 miles south of Edmonton and next to the Hobema Indian Reservation. Would Gordon be willing to come and serve as pastor?

The offer was literally a dream come true. Years earlier, probably about 1957, Gordon had seen a picture of the idyllic, white stucco country church in the rolling hills of the province of Alberta. The photo was hung on the wall of a friend on the mission field in Africa. He remembered commenting that it would be an ideal church to pastor. Now was his chance. Though they had never met Gordon and Geneva, church members asked them to come for several years and help them in what was now a struggle to survive. Seeming community disinterest was eroding support for the church.

Gordon and Geneva prayed about the offer and talked it over. They then replied to the church that they would commit to two years of service, dependent on their recuperation and return to Africa. The church agreed.

Now the question for Gordon and Geneva was how to get there. Decatur County was taking bids on a pickup truck that had been converted and used for ecological surveys. It had a special flatbed and a heated cab on the back.

Gordon went to the County Courthouse and asked, 'What do you think is the lowest bid on it?' Then Gordon put in a bid a bit *lower*.

"It would have to be the Lord getting it for us," Gordon says.

Several months later, the county called him. The truck was his.

Gordon loaded the truck with all their belongings and drove alone to Malmo, Canada, then flew back to Kansas. He and the family made the trip together in a Ford LTD.

They arrived in Malmo during the summer of 1966.

"I'll never forget driving into the church yard with the big, two-story house next to the church," Geneva says. "There was a big wind break of evergreen trees on two sides. To the south, across a slight valley, was a peaceful little cemetery. The sun was bathing everything in light. Big peonies and other flowers were just starting to come out."

The members of the church were eager to meet the new pastor and his family. Some deacons joined them for a big, farm-style dinner with one of the church families, the Bensons. Then they drove over to another family, the Mosesons, where the truck was parked. Then it was on to their new home, the parsonage.

The church had clearly done its best to make a warm home for the Christensens. When they opened the back door, they found a large eat-in kitchen. Two big windows faced south, and two more over the sink helped make the room bright and sunny. Someone had made sure the white curtains, trimmed in aqua, coordinated with white cabinets, also with aqua trim.

The living and dining room smelled new with carpet, and there was a new davenport, or chesterfield to Canadians, and matching chair. A bedroom on the main floor had been converted to a den, which Geneva would eventually decorate with things from Africa, and there also was a shelf-lined office. Below was a full basement with washer and dryer as well as a fruit and vegetable cellar, and upstairs was a master bedroom and two others, one already set up for the girls and the other set up for Michael.

What a home! It was more than they had hoped for. But the church showed its thoughtfulness in more ways than just supplying a nice home. "We all loved it from the very first," Geneva says, "And the very next day Gordon Moseson came with a cute little part-cocker puppy for the children. He had two white front paws, so his name was Mittens."

And the first Sunday, the service was followed by a potluck dinner and then a welcoming food shower. Tables were lined with staples and other foods. "The people were warm and friendly, and they shared liberally of their farm produce with us — cream, milk meat, vegetables," Geneva says. "The young people had planted a big garden for us just a short distance from the house in one of the member's fields. We preserved big cabbages, carrots, potatoes and other root vegetables until way after Christmas in our vegetable cellar."

As the school year rolled around again, Susan enrolled in the high school at Wetaskiwin, the county seat, about 20 miles away. Michael and Mary Lynn were much closer, at the Rosebrier Consolidated School only two miles off, where about 100 children from grades one to nine attended. All the kids did well in their new schools.

Meanwhile, Gordon was learning about the church and this congregation. He decided that the church needed to evangelize to get it growing again. He and a deacon started knocking on farmhouse doors and inviting people. They were met with different responses, including some that were rather calloused spiritually. As usual was the challenge, "Show me a real Christian and I'll believe!" Like so many in the outside world, such people were focused on the negative aspects they saw, or thought they saw, in the believers.

The truck Gordon had bought in Kansas proved to be a key tool in reaching out to the community. With the heater in the back, which ran off the engine, the truck became a perfect Sunday school bus. After adding some benches in the back with the help of a church member, Gordon soon was bringing children from the community and nearby Indian reservation to services. It was an introduction to Christianity much like Gordon had received as a child about 35 years earlier.

Gordon also realized the church needed a revival. He took what he had seen in the revival in Congo during the '50s and put it to work in Canada. Prayer was the beginning. There were regular Bible study and prayer meetings on Wednesday evenings, but it took the emphasis on prayer meetings during the first full week in January 1968 to bring home the truth of the Word of God to somewhat indifferent hearts.

The meetings that week were held in members' homes and attracted more people each night as the week progressed. The Wednesday evening prayer meetings also increased in attendance throughout the month of January and February and into the month of March.

Eventually men, women and children were packing the farm houses for the meetings. A passion for God was being ignited in the hearts of the people. A guest speaker, Cabot Johnson of Helena, Montana, was invited to minister during the week of March 24-31, but a revival had begun before he even arrived.

Mr. Johnson spoke two or three evenings that week, but, Gordon says, "The Lord took over."

"We wouldn't know each night what would transpire," he says. "Singing, then testimonies, then tears and confessions, and people walking around praying for each other. The meetings would go on past midnight.

"Saturday night of that week, a crowd came from neighboring churches, and the downstairs and balcony were all filled," Gordon says. "The Lord had given a promise for that church, and it was from Haggai:

> *I will fill this house with My glory ... and in this place will I give peace.* — Haggai 2:7

"He certainly did that," Gordon says. "Revival is mainly for believers, and differences were resolved and new fires fanned into flames in the lives of many believers."

For the next three months, Gordon and Geneva saw huge changes in the hearts of people. "Time after time we didn't know what the Lord would do next, but He did," Gordon says. "People were being revived."

One woman came to Gordon and said that she had gotten to the point before the revival that she didn't want to hear the phone ring. She didn't care who it was, she wanted nothing to do with them. Now she couldn't wait to tell people what God was doing!

One winter prayer meeting was being held in a postcard-perfect setting; a warm farmhouse with a picture window looking out on great piles of untouched Canadian snow, and the Christensens could sense the power of God moving. A woman stepped forward with four pages of confessions to read. People were praying and manifesting the love of God. It was palpable.

The revival continued into the summer of 1968. In the meantime, Gordon and Geneva were asked, after two years at the church, to return to the mission field that fall. "They had been renewed at the Malmo church, and so had we," Gordon says.

At the final service the Sunday night before the Christensens left, 12 young people came forward and were received into membership. They gave personal testimonies — twice!

The two years in Canada had been another exercise for Gordon in learning keys to spiritual revival. Upon their return to Zaire, Gordon applied them again when he was asked to be a speaker at the church's annual conference in Northwest Zaire.

"I told them, 'Yes, if you will pray every day, from the time you get this letter until the time of the meeting.'"

He knew that nothing could begin without the prayers of the people calling for God's involvement. The people accepted Gordon's offer, and at that Kala Church Conference, another revival began.

Life Lessons

Gordon and Geneva could have looked at two years of pastoring at a smaller church in Canada as an aside in their careers, but it was far from that. "It was a building block, and it certainly wasn't anything negative in our spiritual growth," Gordon says.

It was more evidence for them that God is in any circumstance, able to shape it and use it for our good. When we get to the ends of our lives, a look back can show us how even problems and huge obstacles were useful in His hands.

"We had had a lot of sickness," Geneva says, "and we saw how God had been preparing us for ministry there. When we arrived in Canada, there was one man who was suffering from hepatitis with a lot of depression with it, and Gordon had gone through several bouts of that and could understand that, including the depression. ... He had a real ability to minister to the man because he knew what he was suffering.

"There was another woman in the church that had had bouts of depression with other emotional problems ... she had been going through this stress and strain, and I could understand her problem better. I spent hours with her down at the hospital, and she'd be over at our house. So we could see well that through our illnesses God had prepared us to minister to people, because I think it's difficult to minister to others unless you have some idea of what they might be going through.

"Paul says that in Corinthians. He says we suffer that we may be able to comfort those who are going through sorrow and suffering. Nothing is lost if it is committed into God's hands. Nothing is lost. What value can sickness be? Of great value in the Lord's hands."

Another lesson: Revival is about changing hearts one by one, not media blitzes and programs.

"We can spend zillions of dollars on media announcements and still never experience revival," Gordon says. "Believing, receiving prayer precedes every mighty move of God."

He cites this verse:

> *If my people, which are called by my name, shall humble themselves, and pray, and seek my face, and turn from their wicked ways; then will I hear from heaven, and will forgive their sin, and will heal their land.* — II Chronicles 2:7

In 1968: Susan, Geneva, Michael, Gordon, Mary.

Chapter 14

Music To God's Ears

Returning to Africa in 1968, Gordon and Geneva were stationed at the Bible Institute in Goyongo, where they taught and continued writing pamphlets and Bible study materials. One set of small booklets written at that time proved to be very useful and were still in print in the 1990s. The Christensens called them the "problem" books because they listed scriptures regarding problems that Zairians often faced.

Some of the most important lessons Gordon taught, however, were not in a classroom, but with the school's marching band. The group of 12 to 14 students used second-hand instruments shipped from the states and stored in plywood cases that a missionary carpenter built in Africa. Later they would have uniforms, also gifts from the U.S.

Music had always been a thread running through the Christensens' ministry. Gordon had been introduced to music in the choir of the First Covenant Church in Seattle, as well as the piano lessons Evert Bjordahl had given him as a boy. Gordon also had learned to play trumpet as a student at North Park College.

When Gordon and Geneva had begun teaching in Tandala during the 1950s, a missionary had already formed a chorus and taught the men to sing in parts — quite a feat, since the major tribe had a musical scale of only five notes. By the first class graduation at Tandala in 1955, the chorus sang in unison "A Mighty Fortress is Our God" at the ceremony. The sound of those powerful African voices singing so skillfully was a thrill for music lovers like the Christensens.

But it was the band, first formed in Tandala in 1956 and well-established by the fourth term, that Gordon found most useful as a musical teaching tool. It helped overcome a crippling lack of vision that many Africans suffered. The reason: Death was a constant threat.

"Their traditionally short lifespans affected their whole outlooks," Gordon says. "They could expect to be dead by age 35. So the idea was, 'Don't plant a fruit tree; you'll never eat from it.' ... I think this is why the early colonialists were castigated. 'Why don't you do this or that?' How do you accomplish anything when people are expecting to die tomorrow, or tonight? The mortality rate in those early days had to have been at least 50 percent or more. A measles epidemic would come through, and most of the babies would be gone, like the chickens, which they saw wiped out every year by an epidemic.

"Even when people were regenerated, to get them to cast off this idea of 'My little life' was difficult."

"It went far deeper," Geneva says. "It was a spiritual thing."

"The struggle to survive was so constant that even their new relationships with God took on a utilitarian note," she says. Since the God the missionaries taught about was good and loving, then He was no threat. Thus, they could concentrate on dealing with the threats that surrounded them. Their logic was to ignore the good God and focus on appeasing the evil gods they believed killed their people, destroyed their crops or ruined their hunts.

"As you look at the whole African culture, animistic basically, the people believed that there were spirits all over and about to get them," Gordon says. "They have false gods all around them, and behind every one of them is the devil himself. So they were Satan worshippers. And very often, in the early years, they would take the cream of their youth and they would sacrifice once a year. ... Different tribes did it differently. But if we could have gotten back way in the woods, back in time a couple of centuries, we would have seen they were offering human sacrifices like the Incas."

This fear-filled outlook crept into every part of life.

"Preparing for the birth of a child could be very bad," Geneva says. "They would have no preparation at all. No clothing for them, no clean garment, because you cannot call the attention of the spirits to that child, or they will grab it away."

The same with any preparation for the future, even on such a simple level as planting fruit trees. That was dangerous, the Africans feared. This was like an open challenge to evil spirits, that the people were assuming they could overcome their power, live long lives and someday eat from the trees.

"So when I first talked to a student way back in 1953 or '54, I could see way down the pike, that this was going to develop into a band," Gordon says. "But with their almost tunnel vision, 'We have just a few years at best ....' "

"You did not prepare for the future," Geneva says. "That was one of the great difficulties of working with them, getting them to foresee developing schools and other things."

But building a band was all about planning for the future. It was about developing a skill that could be a year or more away. It demanded practice and discipline. It offered daily victories that could be built upon tomorrow. Through trumpets, drums and trombones, their thinking began to change.

The band also became a status symbol for the school, since it was the only one in that part of Zaire. Other schools had established academic reputations, and the Bible Institute had none.

"Their students had it all over ours," Gordon says. "Ours were not as academically prepared to begin with. But the band gave them status. This was totally unique."

It was also a very effective witnessing tool for the institute. "The villages had never heard anything like this," Gordon says. "It was a powerful tool, very effective, because the music riveted their attention."

Thus, the band provided vision, status, taught organizational skills and perseverance, all traits that had to be built in the students.

The band became a regional sensation, and when government dignitaries would be in the area, the band would usually lead the procession with renditions of "Onward Christian Soldiers" or "Stand Up for Jesus."

But again, for every step of progress, there seemed to be a toll taken on the Christensens. One of the costs of their missions efforts was the family separation of sending the children to boarding school, starting at the age of 7, or second grade.

"That was the hardest part of my missionary career, without exception," Geneva says.

While Gordon and Geneva worked at Goyongo, the children lived at the school in Karawa. The family would be reunited for two weeks in October, two or three weeks at Christmas, two weeks in spring and then summer off.

"Some children could go away to school and not seemingly have any problem," Geneva says. "They left home very casually and could come back. Our children had always been such a definite part of our ministry together, that it was difficult for them to leave home."

By this term, Mary Lynn had reached the fifth grade and was still struggling with leaving home.

While the boarding school was staffed by people deeply committed to these children, they simply could not replace a parent's love and personal guidance. Thus, unbeknown even to the staff, children would often cry themselves to sleep at night. During the day, a child might have seemed adjusted, but for some, the nights were full of tears.

Looking back, Gordon and Geneva see other tolls the system took:

- Gordon could see the time apart from family straining the ties, until Michael, for example, after 10 or 11 weeks at school, would have a tough time adjusting to Gordon as "dad." While Gordon wanted the relationship to resume at a closer level, he could see Michael felt somewhat strange around him the first few days of vacation.

- Geneva missed being with her children at key developmental stages. Not only for emotional fulfillment of being there, but because she knew it was a need in the children's lives. "It can be hard for dorm parents to be sensitive to a child's special spiritual needs at such a time," she says. "We would have liked to have been there, to help them."

That was especially true because of the culture clash the children had to negotiate. Gordon and Geneva say their daughters especially struggled with the inconsistencies of the African "friends" they made, friendships that, as in all things, were more utilitarian than heartfelt. Friendship was a device for getting needs met, just as marriage was a utilitarian rather than emotional relationship. Such an emotional jungle, heaped on top of the insecurity caused by separation from Mom and Dad, was a severe test for the girls.

- Regardless of a child's readiness at a young age, the mission system nevertheless expected those children to be sent off to Karawa so the mothers could be focused on mission work. "It traumatized some of the children," Gordon says. "The parents, too."

These issues cut to the core of what Geneva cherished. Family had always been a key to her life. For her, family unity was essential to overcoming life's hardships, whether a childhood in Dust Bowl Kansas or the extreme rigors of missionary life in remote Zaire.

"I knew I could get through anything, as long as my family was okay. As long as my children were happy and cared for," Geneva says. "Concerns for them weighed more heavily on me than any challenge I faced personally in Africa."

But Geneva can see how God had forewarned her of this unforeseeable challenge years before she got on the field. Through the stories of people she encountered while a nursing student, she was being braced for what was to come. There was the girl who had spent her childhood in boarding schools and became afraid of meeting her missionary parents. There was the girl who stayed in the U.S. and spent only furloughs with her parents, but her mother died while she was young.

Geneva learned the lesson. When she did end up a missionary parent, she and Gordon worked as best they could to overcome the temptation to neglect, only a day at a time, their family priorities in order to do missions work. The method of the devil often is to slowly creep into life and divert priorities just for a day — until the days are weeks, then months, years, and finally an entire childhood. They battled it with:

- Prayer, of course. Their children were daily in their prayer lives.

- Family time when possible. Gordon didn't plan missions trips when the kids were home on break, so they would be together.
- When they saw one of their daughters was not doing well, they brought her home despite the expectations that she be in the boarding school. The break from school for homeschooling awhile helped her get her feet back under her and to go back later.
- They talked to their children about it. Keeping the channels of communication open helped a lot, because the understanding helped the children overcome any haunting "whys?"

"As our son said, 'We knew you weren't just putting us down there to get rid of us, that it was a matter of necessity,'" Geneva says.

Gordon and Geneva also found many positive elements to the boarding school experience. One was very pragmatic: The children received excellent medical care at Karawa, better than they could have gotten in Goyongo. They were safer at the school. But there were other considerations as well that they say reflect very positively on the Karawa school in particular:

- The teachers, dorm parents and staff that Karawa attracted were truly committed to scripture. Though they couldn't replace parents, they were caring, loving guardians who became "aunts" and "uncles" to all the children. They made excellent role models.
- It was clearly a Christian school, run by missionary teachers who emphasized things like scripture memory and Godly values. "However you cut the cake, at home or abroad, if they do not memorize scripture, if they do not have it hidden deep in their hearts, these kids are not going to make it spiritually," Gordon says. "They have got to have

a reserve in their computers, so that at any moment, it can pop up and be of help to them. This was marvelous."

- The children learned to live in community, having some responsibility no matter what age. A healthy work ethic and self discipline were engrained in children.
- The children were sharing in the mission of their parents. On Sundays or weekdays they would go out on missions projects or play sports with the Africans. They spent time in villages, gave testimonies, taught Sunday school classes. They developed a heart for the lost.
- Educationally, socially and spiritually, they had more advantages than the average child who lives in the U.S. Gordon noted that Susan once told him that in retrospect, despite the boarding school setting, she had more family time as a boarder than children who live with their parents in the U.S. In the U.S., where the average adult male spends one minute per day with his child (though newer studies show that number improving), Gordon's two weeks out of every 10 or 11, as well as the summers, allowed them to get a lot in. Again, this had to be a decision by Gordon and Geneva in order to happen, and Geneva thanks the Lord for his early warning to her to guard her family in the midst of "the work."
- The children developed a lifelong extended family through the boarding school. The teachers, dorm parents and other children were drawn closely together by living as well as learning together. They have a bond that is evident as they go on in life, often working together on the mission field they grew up on.

- The cross-cultural experience, the international travel, the global world view that resulted from their childhoods as missionary kids are rare jewels. In fact, Gordon and Geneva say, the "deprived" childhood that their children supposedly endured as missionary kids is actually envied by their peers who grew up in suburbia. It's a life full of adventure, purpose and meaning. When you've grown up this way, it's hard to live a life dedicated to getting a bigger house or a home theater electronic system.

In the meantime, things have changed on the mission field. The Evangelical Covenant Church has listened and responded to the concerns of missionary parents. Whereas the missions program was not supportive of homeschooling and expected children to be boarded, the program is fully supportive now. Children may go to boarding school when they and the parents feel the time is right. As a result, many of the missionaries on the field today, who were missionary kids and grew up in the Karawa school, are homeschooling their children in the early years. To Gordon and Geneva, the fact that the children went back to the mission field says something positive about their childhood experiences, while the fact that they are choosing to homeschool suggests they are trying to prevent something in their children's lives that they experienced.

"By waiting until a kid is ready, eager, and wants to go to the school, the biggest problem evaporates," Gordon says.

Also new for the Christensens in the fourth term, and a great addition to their work, was the introduction of private planes to the field.

The missionary work was able to reach much deeper, and much more efficiently thanks to the arrival of Missionary Aviation Fellowship. MAF, based in Redlands, Calif., is an independent ministry of civilian aviators who seek through air travel to help missionaries and African church leaders.

"It was revolutionary," Geneva says of the air ministry. "It opened up schooling. We could get back and forth to our kids. ... They could even come home for some weekends."

It also made the medical work much more efficient. In some medical emergencies, a missions doctor might have to get in a truck and spend many hours on rough jungle roads getting to an emergency case. With the airplane and several strategic airstrips, their assistance could be only an hour away.

This took a huge burden off Geneva, who as a station nurse often had to make very heavy decisions about how to treat a patient. "It was a very big decision to start the trek to the hospital at Karawa rather than deal with a case at the station."

Now with the airplane, she could share some of that burden with doctors who were more accessible.

Yet almost immediately upon the arrival of the air service, Geneva learned that it would never replace God on the mission field.

The lesson came in the form of a medical emergency in 1968. The Christensens had just arrived from Canada, and the children hadn't even started the fall school term yet at Karawa.

"One morning the kids came running in and said, 'Aunty Joy is calling for you right away.'"

It was Joy Lundquist. They were next door neighbors on the station, and her 7-year-old son, Paul, was about to start his first year at Karawa.

When Geneva got to the Lundquist's house, she found Paul on the davenport having convulsions. Joy told her that the plane was in flight, picking up people for a conference.

"The plane had picked up Don Lundquist, Paul's father, at Goyongo, and had, I think, Dr. Gordon Johnson on board already. They probably hadn't been gone more than 30 minutes when we radioed them."

Geneva described Paul's condition: subnormal temperature and continuing convulsions.

The plane turned around and started back for Goyongo.

"This was amazing to me," Geneva says. "Susan and the kids were gathered at our house, praying. As we heard the plane coming in, we lost all vital signs on Paul. He was done in. He had started out with strong convulsions, but before he would come out of them. This time, he just went out.

"I looked at Bibs (missionary nurse Bergith Seashore), whom I had sent the kids for, and she looked at me. We didn't say a word to Joy. She was standing near the radio, keeping in contact with the plane. And I thought, 'Oh, Lord, they are so close! Is he going to die as they are landing?' And it was revealed to me that I had a lot of faith in the doctor coming and not enough faith in God, as I had had to do before.

"I could not get any pulse. I could not get anything.

"I told Susan and Michael to take the pickup to the airstrip and get the people. They picked them up and came roaring up the hill. And I'll never forget Don Lundquist stepping in the door. He was the first one to come in, of course, to see his little boy. And Paul opened his eyes and said, 'Hi, Dad!' And I thought, 'What have we just witnessed here?' No thrashing around, no coming out of this convulsion as he had before. He just opened his eyes and said, 'Hi, Dad.'

"And that was it. The doctor was absolutely unnecessary."

As they started tracking down the problem, Joy told them that Paul had said something that morning about being bitten on the leg by something. When Joy was making the bed later, she found the leg of a tarantula spider. Later that week she found a tarantula, minus one leg, in her kitchen.

"Why he didn't succumb, why he just opened his eyes ... that was a new era for me," Geneva says. "To have the use of the airplane like that, but to realize, 'No, you are still dependent on God, airplane or no airplane.'"

There were other times that the lesson came home that the plane was a blessing, but God was still God.

"Michael had been sick down at school, but he hadn't told us," Geneva says. "He came home and I didn't realize how sick he was. Michael was one of few words.

"One night I heard a strange noise, and it was Michael trying to call us. He was having trouble breathing. I pulled up a chair and sat with him all night. He pulled and pushed for every breath he had. I listened to his chest, and it was like listening to an old, wheezing pump organ. I couldn't discern anything. It was just noise.

"The next morning, as soon as the radio was open, I called into Karawa, and they got Dr. Roger Thorpe on. I told him what was going on, and he said, 'I'll be right there.'

"That again was a real blessing of that airplane. He got up there fast. He examined him, and he had severe pericarditis. His liver was inflamed, the lining of his lungs and internal organs seemed to be inflamed and rubbing on each other. Dr. Thorpe left some medication and told me to take his blood pressure every half hour.

"Michael could not feed himself, he could not do a thing. He was struggling for his life."

"With each of our kids, the Lord allowed each to come to the point where we had to say, 'There is nothing medically we can do for these kids. We put them back in your hands.' It was another time when we were absolutely cast on the Lord. Now why the Lord spared him and some others didn't get spared, we don't know. The Lord certainly tested our faith at the time."

"But Michael was so positive all the time. Gordon would come near the door, and he kind of panics when he sees someone in real severe physical distress, and Michael would gaspingly laugh at him. But it hurt him so bad, so we had to kind of keep Gordon out of the way."

Michael did come out of it. He went back to school after his recovery, resuming the 10th grade.

Meanwhile, Susan had finished school and was preparing to return to the U.S. to begin college. She first spent a year on the field, working with Gordon and Geneva, organizing preschool for students' children in Goyongo. Then she enrolled at Tabor College in Kansas, majoring in education.

For Susan, college was another time of culture shock. Gordon had always explained to his children that they would always be culturally different from those around them, and that was okay. They were not fully American, because of their African experience. But they were not Africans either. That explained a lot of the strange behaviors they saw in African children that did not fit what they had been taught.

But Susan found fitting into America was not easy, either. The priorities of the girls she met at college were very different. They were very involved, for example, in clothes and cultivating certain relationships.

Geneva sums it up with, "Their world seemed small."

"She could not relate to the kids very well," Geneva says. "She finally roomed with a Kenyan at her college, and she helped Susan adjust to her own culture, because she had been there a few years. She helped Susan more than anyone else could have."

"One day, this girl said, 'Susan, you are just a little black girl in a white skin!' which kind of shows you where Susan was coming from. But this Kenyan girl understood this, so she was a tremendous help to Susan."

"It was funny," Gordon says. "A Kenyan, who had to go through all that adjustment, helping a missionary kid make the adjustment."

But it wasn't long before Susan had more support in the states.

She had been in the U.S. about a year when the fourth term ended for Gordon and Geneva. They could look back and see a lot of accomplishments, but there was more to accomplish at home. It had been dawning on Gordon during this term that he had to do something about a very strained relationship from way back. He was thinking of his father. They had been at odds since he was born again at age 10. It was time to try and right things.

So in 1972, the Christensen family left Zaire for furlough and moved to Seattle, Washington.

Life Lessons

Gordon and Geneva look back on these years and catalog the big lessons they learned in short sentences:

- Our times are in God's hands.
- God wants to be sure He is our first love.
- Inventions and improvements can never take the place of God.
- God is on His almighty throne, and He can work when no one else can.

Chapter 15

Spiritually Filled To Overflowing

Like the boy David in the Old Testament, Gordon Christensen had been facing lions and bears ever since he was a kid. He had been born into a hard world, with a hard father who, beset with lifelong problems of his own, had become a powerful opponent of his son.

He didn't approve of his son's involvement in church. Of his time spent with church people. Of his desire to pursue a career in Christian ministry instead of a career that offered prestige and money.

In short, Ivor Christensen had stood against his son almost all his life.

It's very tough for a little boy to go up against a father who is telling you, "You are wrong. You are wrong, You are wrong." It's confusing to have a father you love but, nevertheless, you know by the time you are 10 cannot be your role model.

Gordon and his father had much unresolved when Gordon left home for college. In the ensuing years, they almost never saw each other. On the few occasions when Gordon did bring his family back to meet their relatives in Washington, it was a disaster. Gordon would have to lay down edicts like, "No alcohol" on a road trip to see some sight in the state. Otherwise, the pattern Gordon had known since childhood would repeat itself: a festive family gathering dissolving into a drinking party.

Decades had passed since Gordon had spent anything but superficial time with his parents, and he was feeling a tug at his heart about his father. Ivor had received some warnings from his doctor that he had to stop drinking alcohol, or it was going to kill him. But Gordon knew that alcohol was only anesthetizing longstanding emotional wounds Ivor had suffered, wounds that had alienated him from God. Gordon hoped that he could win his father to the Lord.

The occasion came during the furlough of 1972-74. Gordon and Geneva moved back to Seattle with Mary Lynn and Michael, and Susan went to college at Seattle Pacific.

It was a great family time and an opportunity for Mary Lynn and Michael to experience life off the mission field. And Gordon and Geneva were there to help, day by day. For the Christensens, it was a great time of being together.

There was another parallel between Gordon's life and the Old Testament's David that would become manifest in the next two years. God was going to show Gordon and Geneva another Goliath, the Goliath of the spiritual realm, and teach them how to fight him.

It was a lesson Gordon and Geneva had sensed was needed, but they had never been able to put their finger on it. They had both seen unexplainable phenomena among the African people — phenomena that would chill them to the core. And they felt inadequate to confront them. They had just seen and sensed from time to time that they were up against something very big, much bigger than they were ready to handle.

That is another reason the years 1972-'74, Midway Covenant Church in Seattle, and its pastor, the Rev. Fred Neth, became so important to Gordon and Geneva.

After some time of learning at Midway about ministering in the Spirit, Pastor Fred got ahold of a very unusual tape. It purported to be a recording of an actual exorcism conducted in Texas. A woman who had spent years in a mental hospital was brought to this pastor for help, and he tape recorded the proceedings.

Gordon recalls the tape with a chuckle.

"You can't believe the ignorance of some of these demons. Some of us give them too much credit for being smart. But they said to this pastor, 'Pastor, if you will lay off, I will make you rich. I have done it for a lot of people. I will make you rich. Look at your shoes. You could have new shoes all the time. Look at that suit. I could put a brand new suit on you, if you will just lay off.'

"The pastor responded, 'I know who you are. You are an emissary from the devil himself. And I rebuke you in Jesus' name!' And these 19 (demons) came screaming out."

The tape was a kind of window — and early alert — on how ministry at Midway was going to change.

However, the ground was prepared at Midway Covenant Church long before it became a battleground for open spiritual warfare. The process had begun with a boyhood friend of Gordon's, Roy Lindquist, part of that dance-hall Sunday school outreach that had also changed Gordon's life decades ago. Roy led many to Christ and developed a good nucleus of Godly people in Midway Covenant Church. He was a spirit-led, evangelistic developer pastor who laid a solid foundation for Pastor Fred.

Also, the times were right for Midway Church, Gordon explained:

"Some of the background to Midway's story was also the background of our American culture. We had just come through the '60s, where everything was called into question. And spiritual life was certainly on the decline, and God always raises up antithesis to the thesis. One of the ways He did this was the Jesus Movement.

"At this time I was reading Francis Scheaffer's book, *The Church at the End of the 20th Century*, and it stirred me to the depths. He recalled some of his experiences at L'Abri, in Switzerland, and told about welcoming people into their home, who at times set fire to the drapes through some of their habits, and soiled the house. And this was his main theme: that the church at the end of the 20th century has to welcome every and any person, no matter where they've been or where they are, or where we think they ought to be.

"So that challenged me to the quick. Then to see the Jesus People welcomed and feeling right at home, occupying some of the front seats of the church, sometimes shouting 'Amen,' standing with their arms outstretched — it encouraged me to see God raising up a whole new force to battle the indifference and lethargy, to do spiritual warfare."

Midway was anything but a conventional Covenant Church. On this occasion when Gordon preached there, he told people to stand, shake a hand and say 'Praise the Lord!'

"I felt such release to be myself and to let people be themselves and enjoy fellowship. It was a marvelous time."

Gordon was usually busy traveling to other churches on weekends, but he was involved in Midway's weekday services. And he saw active development of lay ministry. "It was learning the pastor does not do it all," Gordon says.

Amid this willingness to change at the church, a church problem came to Pastor Fred's attention and needed his involvement. A church member needed confrontation — again — over promiscuity.

"This woman was afflicted with two things," Gordon says. "She was lustful to the core. She said she couldn't help herself. Also, she was in total confusion. Her checking account, for example, was a disaster.

"So the pastor called her in and said, 'This has got to be it. We have warned you repeatedly.'"

The woman told the pastor that she knew she was doing wrong, but she could not help herself.

"The pastor said, 'You *can* help yourself. If you had a loaded gun to your head, you tell me you couldn't control yourself.' She said, 'The illustration doesn't apply. I am out of control.'

"So Pastor Neth told her, 'All right, there is one last prayer.' And if he had known what was going to happen, he would have called in all the deacons, anybody who had any spiritual inkling of what might transpire. At any rate, they went into the church with the church secretary, but she knew nothing about this, either. So they were kneeling there and Pastor Neth prayed a very innocent little prayer, He said, 'Lord, if there something here that we don't know anything about ...' and BANG! The woman took off. I mean blasphemy and screaming. Pastor Fred commanded: "In the name of Jesus, tell me your name!" And the first one was lust. So he said, 'In Jesus' name, I command you, lust, to come out of her.'

The experience left them shocked and exhausted. It had gone on for several minutes. In the midst of this exorcism, the woman had gotten sick and vomited in the sanctuary. But the lust that had plagued this woman was gone.

Pastor Neth held a second session with the woman and cast out a demon that called itself confusion.

"She was back on target," Gordon says of the woman.

There was no turning back for Fred. There was no denying or explaining away this encounter with the demonic realm. The things we often wonder about this "enemy of men's souls" that is described in the Bible, these stories about Jesus casting out demons, or these Old Testament passages about "The devil walking to and fro in the earth," were very real at that time. They were not allegories, euphemisms or colorful descriptions of man's own evil nature or mental illness. They were literal and accurate. And Pastor Fred realized he was being called off the bench and into the middle of this spiritual contest.

A revolution was under way at Midway Covenant Church, the opening shots apparently fired long before any of the people had realized it. But now Pastor Fred clearly saw that he and his people had a fight on their hands.

The weekday services took a different tack from the Sunday morning services.

"We are a mainline church," Gordon says of the Covenant. "We have some traditionalists who want the Lord's Prayer at a certain point in the program, and "don't touch it" is their motto. But this was, of course, absolutely left field. The pastor believed in the baptism of the Holy Spirit. People were standing up in church and saying, 'I've been baptized in the Holy Spirit,' and the old timers are saying, 'What do you mean by that?'"

Geneva says, "During the midweek service, there was speaking in tongues, etc., and Pastor Fred was really qualified to lead at that time, because he really had the spirit of discernment, and if anybody thought they had a message in tongues, and it was not, he immediately sat them down. He ran a tight ship on that."

"He promoted the spiritual manifestations, but absolutely refused to allow froth. And the church was going forward. Is still going forward."

The changes didn't go unnoticed by the hierarchy of the Covenant Church. Many longtime Covenanters found the changes at Midway frightening and too strange. Many left, as Pastor Fred put it, "for safer ground." But as they left, they talked about what was going on at Midway to the denomination's leaders.

What Gordon and Geneva saw going on thrilled and energized them. The earlier church emphasis on lay ministry, on the pastor not having to do it all, was taking on new, more powerful dimensions.

"These people were being prepared for ministry," Gordon says. "Some were being prepared for healing ministry. Others for leading people into a deeper prayer fellowship with the Lord. And there were those who had a gift of prophetic utterance, and they were attracted to that, because God's spirit was drawing them, just like a moth to the flame. Because he was building a new fellowship, all centered around the spirit's direction and gifts."

This was the power Gordon and Geneva had seen such need for during their years in Zaire. At Midway, power-filled Christian believers were impacting their society by simply living in it while being obedient to God. This way, they were affecting the culture rather than being affected by it.

For example, two members of the Midway Church were passing a large party at a neighborhood home when they felt led by the spirit to stop and witness to the people there.

"They didn't know how," Gordon says, "so they walked in, started talking to people, and asked, 'Can we tell you about something very important, our faith in Christ?'"

Gordon says people let them proceed without any problem. "By that time the people had enough beer in them, and it was fine."

While they were working their way through the house talking to people, a woman's scream brought the party to a standstill. "A lady cries, 'I've lost my diamond!'" Gordon says. It was somewhere near her car, dropped in the dark.

"The spirit of God came on these two men," Gordon says. "One of them is the dad of Brad Hill, who has written the books Soul Graft and Splinters from the Cross about his missionary experiences in Zaire. He said, 'Listen, everybody! Now we are going to show you that what we're talking about is for real. God is going to produce that diamond ring.'"

The men prayed, joined hands and then started walking backwards toward the street. They got to the the gutter when one of the men, John Gettis, simply leaned down and picked the ring up without even having to look for it.

The two already had gotten everyone's full attention. Now everyone was stunned. Gordon says John Gettis told his rapt audience, "'There it is! Now you know God is here and God is speaking to you!'"

It was a miraculous witness, the kind almost never seen or experienced. But it was the result of a momentum that was building at Midway Covenant Church. More and more such things were happening in that congregation. With each sign and wonder, the people got stronger in their faith, until, as in the above episode, people could be going along their way and believe God really was calling them to go into a party and witness for Him.

"This wasn't something that just hit them," Gordon says. "They had seen miracle after miracle. Their believing was such that anything was possible.

"Things were happening all the time. The church should have written a book."

This didn't happen without a lot of turmoil and strife. People were leaving the church over it. New people were coming because of it. The church was reshaping and seemed to be spinning far from its denominational roots.

Or, perhaps, it was returning to them. The Covenant Church's beginnings date to the 1800s in Sweden, where the Lutheran Church was and still is the state church. To many in those early days, the church seemed to have become more of a tool of the state bureaucracy than a house of God.

At that time, there was a national push to improve literacy, and consequently, a bigger market for literature developed. Traveling book salesmen were setting off to make sales among the tough, simple farm families now making rapid gains in education. Those salesmen found the best seller to be the bestseller of all time, the Bible. Family Bible studies began to sprout in the countryside, with farm families gathering in homes with their neighbors to explore the Bible. This hadn't been done at all in the state church. The Bible was new ground for these farmers.

What they learned seemed to put them at odds with the church and caused friction. For one thing, the family Bible times did not have state sanction. That made the farmers sort of outlaws. Covenanters were derisively called "The Readers" because of their seemingly naive attention to the Bible. That definitely made them unfashionable as well. Also, they usually were poor people who had little social status anyway.

It was in the migrations to the U.S. Midwest in the mid- and late-1800s that those Swedish immigrants brought their

Bible faith with them to the farms they were founding. Before long, the small Bible groups consisting of perhaps a few families began to realize they could accomplish more by uniting. Their main focus was the big Christian challenge of the era — taking the gospel into newly opened China. Therefore, many of the Swedish immigrants convened in the late 1800s in Chicago and made a pact of Christian unity, or a "covenant," to work together and win China for Christ. It was from that covenant that the denomination drew its name.

Thus, the Covenant's roots were long in evangelism and Bible learning, attracting people who embraced the Bible's teachings, had a desire to impact their world for Christ and could face social criticism.

Perhaps the "new people" showing up at Midway were closer to the Covenant's roots than some second- or third-generation members who had become members out of family tradition. Nevertheless, Covenant leaders were very concerned about this movement into uncharted waters.

It was a time of great personal crisis for Fred Neth. A conference was arranged — but not held — to meet with him in Denver. Later, he was asked to come to Chicago and meet with the church's top administrators.

Pastor Fred did go to Chicago, where he was treated as a consultant on this new move of the spirit being seen in some Covenant churches, but Gordon says also to let top leaders get a good look at him.

"He did feel he was on the hot seat," Gordon says. "A lot of the superintendents were very nervous about such things as public healing meetings, speaking in tongues and prophetic utterances. If there were any restrictions such as, 'None of this in public worship services,' the restrictions certainly came from the superintendents' offices. And not every pastor had the depth and experience that Fred Neth had. Some experienced divisiveness and never recuperated. Often the leadership tried to keep a lid on it, didn't know how to deal with it; it caused a tsunami."

While the Covenant was trying to determine what was going on in its U.S. churches, Gordon and Geneva refused to be distracted by the turmoil. Years of experience had taught them not to get too off course from the spiritual lessons God was teaching them.

In 1974, their furlough came to a close. Gordon and Geneva felt as if they had been in mid-career advanced studies. They had seen enough in Africa to know the problems and challenges. They had seen the problems they could solve with their initial training, and where their early preparations had not equipped them for what they would encounter. But God had been faithful to them through the years. He had shown them, walked with them in it, and now, they felt, He had trained them for deeper ministry.

So Gordon and Geneva didn't spend much time watching Covenant leadership sort out the Midway experience. They were busy packing their spiritual backpacks with this new, better-than-survival gear they saw God handing them. They were enthused, eager and ready to return.

In August 1974, Gordon and Geneva returned to the Bible Institute. Susan and Michael stayed in the U.S. Mary Lynn returned to the Covenant boarding school in Africa.

And Gordon got to work with his new material. He introduced a Bible course on demonology.

LIFE LESSONS

Gordon and Geneva learned that spiritual power need not be reflected in size or numbers.

"Power is not synonymous with bigness or any of the other evaluations of power popularly given today: 'We have seven services going, with 50,000 attending.' The big thing is sacrifice. That is power. Is there humility? That is power. Is there really surrender to the Lord? That is power. Is the spirit speaking, or is somebody else speaking?

"We heard a fellow the other week from Great Britain. He said, 'I have been in church after church in the United States, and I come out empty and angry.' He had been raised where Martin Lloyd Jones was the pastor — excellent pastor. He would see no one an hour before he preached. Deacons could take care of any problem, greet the prime minister if need be. But he came out anointed every time. The British fellow said that was what is missing, why the church sounds so empty. That is what we tried to take to Africa."

Chapter 16

A New War In Africa

"Please don't teach that course again, Mr. Christensen. Bad things happen to us when you teach that course!"

Gordon and Geneva recall with laughter how their introduction of demonology studies did not get a warm greeting. But they were determined to start applying what they had learned, especially in the area of warfare praying.

Gordon used as his basic text a book named *The Fall of the Oppressor* by Francis Ray, a minister who discussed his experiences in Switzerland.

In one of the four concrete block classrooms in Goyongo, Gordon started laying out for about 20 of his students the fundamentals of spiritual warfare, including:

- We have a powerful enemy.
- His power is limited.
- Calvary conquered Satan and his cohorts.
- Nevertheless, Christians must exercise faith in order to withstand his attacks.

As the students pointed out, it was not a topic to be treated lightly. There seemed to be immediate consequences to any efforts at exposing the devil's presence, tactics and weaknesses. At first, problems such as sicknesses began to crop up at the school. Several students had accidents such as cuts, falls and bruises. Several had sudden financial crises that seemed to threaten their Bible school training.

But by the end of the first five-week session on demonology, the students were reporting positive results. The students went out on the field for two-week internships, and one came back with a story of meeting up with demon-possessed people in the village he worked in.

"Without that course, he would have had no recourse but to run from the problem," Geneva says. "Instead, he could help."

Incidents such as casting out demons of fear and anger began building confidence in the students. Bible study suddenly took on a much more practical, immediate value. Here was a survival skill that they were seeing in use, and it could free their people from a lot of oppression they suffered.

The Bible Institute continued on routinely: Gordon taught Bible courses along with Dick Anderson and Don Lundquist. Geneva and Joy Lundquist were teaching women at Goyongo. Geneva joined Gordon whenever possible on the mission trips. Mary Lynn was back at UBAC missionary school.

Gordon and Geneva's official assignment was Wasolo. There hadn't been missionaries there since the 1964 rebellion, when Dr. Paul Carlson was taken.

"The area was in real need spiritually," Geneva says. "However, there was a lack of teachers at Goyongo, so we divided our time."

One surprise of the year was a large gift from a Covenant Church in Minneapolis, Brookdale Covenant, which wanted to help with an evangelistic thrust into unreached territory. The church's gift of $3,750 was to be used in part to reopen Bumba, a port city on the Zaire River between Lisala and Kisanqani. The Covenant Church had a work there and outreach to the surrounding region, but the missionary living quarters had been wrecked during the rebellion and needed to be rebuilt.

The gift also was to be used for cutting-edge ministry.

Several months before the church's gift arrived, Gordon had met a man named Mbangiye (pronounced Bang-QUEE) who had asked, 'When are you going to go to my people, the Pakabeti?' Mbangiye had made a three-day trek from deep in the jungle to a Big Sunday service. At the time, Gordon recalls, his first thought was, "fat chance." The Pakabeti were in such remote territory that he never thought he would get that far into the bush. But when the money arrived, Gordon talked to Doko, the president of the church and director of the Bible Institute, about going to the Pakabeti, and they agreed.

An evangelistic thrust into the Pakbeti Jungle became one of the big projects of the year.

They started April 6, 1975, on a three-day trip to reach the Pakbetis. The first leg of the trip they made by truck, from Goyongo to the river port town of Businga and on toward Lesala. Midway, they detoured down a rough road and into deep jungle. They passed several coffee plantations during their hours of rough travel, but other than that, there was nothing out there. Finally, the road ran out, and the team of about 22 had to leave the trucks and start hiking.

It had not yet started raining, but the weather made for a hot, muggy walk on a narrow forest path. Packing their gear, and Gordon, wearing tennis shoes ("I wasn't well supplied for that kind of hike" he says), they walked an hour or more until they came to a stream. They waded upstream for about one-half kilometer to the Mongala River. It was near nightfall when they crossed the river in dugout canoes and reached a totally non-Christian village, where they stayed in mud huts.

"We had sent in word previously that we were coming, but when we got to the hut on the river, we found our letter. That was as far as it had gotten. So the people had no clue we were coming. Then up a hill on foot, over grassland and into virgin forest." The hike to the Pakabetis totaled about 24 kilometers.

When they reached the Pakabeti region, they passed two large poles, driven into the ground on each side of the path and looking like a portal into another area. On the poles, Gordon was told, were the placentas from the birth of twins, a very bad omen in the region.

It fit the reputation of the Pakabeti, who were a banished people because they were so unruly. The Belgians had forced them into the area of remote jungle because they were such a problem to govern. These were forgotten people in a forgotten place. The territory they lived in, the Monveda Jungle, had not even been mapped.

Finally Gordon's team came upon a typical African jungle village; square and round mud houses, widely spaced apart, which sat in a clearing surrounded by dense, green jungle. As the group approached, Gordon could see the people stoking outdoor fires to start the evening meal, which normally consisted of cooked, pounded green plantains and some kind of meat, ranging from turtle to elephant.

"We got there about 4:30 in the afternoon. It was quite an experience. They had seen a Catholic priest before, but I was the first Protestant they had ever seen.

"That was the longest foot hike I had ever taken in Africa," Gordon says. "The skin was coming off my feet. With about 22 people in our group, it was more like an invasion than an evangelistic tour. ... When we started out on Day Three, they sent out word ahead that we were on the way. When we were an hour or two from their village, they came out to greet us and help us carry baggage and other equipment.

"The people's most distinctive feature was that they were black-black," Gordon says. "Africans divide themselves into black and brown. But these were black-black, beyond the standard definition. They were the blackest Africans I had ever seen. Not all of them, but some of them, and the rest were just plain black, like Mbangiye, who had come out to see us and asked, 'When will you come to our village?'"

A few months after meeting Mbangiye and figuring he would never reach that far into the jungle, Gordon was standing in one of the Pakabetis' villages. "All I can say is

God sure answers prayer. People were praying, 'Let the missionaries come.'"

The plan was to evangelize three villages in the region, Ngakpo, the first they had reached, Bokwele and Bosesi, the village of Mbangiye.

In Ngakpo, most noticeable to Gordon was a constant noise. "There was drumming, dancing all night, people high on marijuana that they grew themselves," Gordon says. "Kids as young as 13, 14, tromped around like they owned the world because they were high on dope. A lot of arguing going on. Then there were these possessed people screaming away."

He was stuck there amid chaos, forced to wait while his feet healed.

But the team began to evangelize in Ngakpo. There were about 200 in the village, because hunters had returned to the area to wait out the dry season. The team would walk through the village, and at night, when more men came back, they would go and sit with them by the fires.

That week there were 35 conversions — and there was less noise. Gordon says the lower volume was the most obvious change in Ngakpo in that one-week stay. Gordon says it had been such mayhem that he couldn't even sleep at night. By the end of the week, he could.

They visited the next two villages the next week.

"The evangelistic plan was to visit each house in the evenings when the hunters would get home," Gordon says. "In one village, 35 responded to the invitations to receive Christ. There were some in the other villages, too. At this time it was difficult to know just how much they had understood, but in subsequent visits, it was evident that lives had been changed."

After that trip into the Monveda Jungle, Gordon and Geneva continued their work as visiting instructors, doing three-month teaching assignments in Goyongo and Wasolo. They also joined in efforts to launch a seminary by extension, using course material already utilized on Free Church and Covenant fields.

"We went to a central village in an area, and the students came for a day of testing on the materials they had studied," Geneva says. "They also received new materials to work for another two weeks. At Wasolo and Abuzi, some students with their wives came a two-day journey by foot! Often, they carried babies, too."

In Wasolo, one of the Covenant's newest areas of work, they found the problem of demonic activity particularly acute.

"That was a learning experience," Gordon says. "We learned to ask, 'What was the original sin that let the demons in?'"

That paved the way to finding what Gordon and Geneva say is the most common route to demonization — bitterness.

They saw many healings:

- A young man came asking for prayer for an extremely painful leg. He walked with the help of a stick. After calling the family together to confess their sins toward one another, which lasted about an hour and a half, it was easy to pray for the young man, and he was healed.

- One day as Gordon and Geneva were passing through a village, a young man came running out and asked for prayer for his mother. As they stepped into her hut, they saw a very sick woman suffering from a distended abdomen. She was lying on her bamboo bed. Gordon laid hands on her and prayed that God's will be done in her life. Shortly afterward, when they were passing through the village again, the family came running out with a huge papaya for Gordon and Geneva. The well mother was standing beside the road.

- At a pastors' and deacons' seminar in the Bumba area that was also attended by the wives, many came with physical needs. As prayer was offered for one another, they were healed. One young pastor had a badly swollen leg from his foot to above the knee, and it was covered with blisters. The next day the leg was fine, and he was rejoicing.

The years 1974-77 were turning into years of miracles.

While these events were going on at established sites, the Pakabetis were trying to open up their area to the missionaries. They had indicated they wanted an airstrip, a dispensary and a pastor. Gordon responded that if they would lay out an airstrip, the mission would help by supplying hoes, machetes, wheel barrows. It was the beginning of an ongoing relationship — a relationship that within 10 years meant a dispensary, airstrip and pastor for the Pakabetis.

The accomplishments were not without challenge, probably the biggest spiritual challenge Gordon and Geneva ever encountered.

On a return trip to the Pakabeti region, Gordon didn't have to hike in in tennis shoes. But the trip into the remote Monveda Jungle could still be strenuous. The airstrip the Pakabetis cut in the jungle was "inadequate," Gordon says. On one trip, he had to get out and give the plane a running push by the wing strut and then jump into the passenger seat before the plane went airborne!

The Pakabetis became a good training spot for the Bible Institute's students. Gordon, Geneva and a group would fly in for on-the-field practice. On one trip, Gordon and a group of five students were ferried in on several flights to the airstrip.

When they got there, they quickly learned they had stepped knee-deep into trouble.

The area was served by Mbangiye, who was now a pastor. He and some of the village's Christians had been praying for a dying girl who was being cared for in Mbangiye's hut.

The whole village was a tinderbox ready to ignite in interfamily warfare. The girl's family was convinced that another family had put a hex on her. When Gordon and several of his students went in the hut, there stacked against the wall were spears and war weapons that Mbangiye had confiscated from the two families, but he knew he didn't have them all. If this girl died, the other weapons would come out. Gordon and the pastor went to the girl and started commanding demons to come out of her, and she did get some deliverance. She perked up from what appeared to be near death, but she still needed a lot of help.

However, she was only part of the problem, Mbangiye said. There were four other people in the village that were possessed, terrorizing the village. He said they needed to spend a day of fasting and prayer, and then get to work. Gordon and Geneva agreed. That was Saturday, the day of their arrival by plane.

Gordon encountered one of these women, the wife of the village church's choir director, one afternoon at the church. Gordon had known this woman had problems with depression before and had seen her getting worse. On one visit, he had found her so depressed that she lay curled up in a fetal position.

But on this day, she went berserk in the church yard. She started barking and howling with what Gordon described as unworldly sounds, and she leaped around like a wild animal. Gordon had tried to help her earlier, commanding the demons to release her, but it was not effective. Within three minutes, he was exhausted.

After the fasting and prayer, the demons started responding to the commands of students to release the woman. These five students, brought in on what was supposed to be a short hop for practical training, were going to get a life's worth in the next several days.

Monday, the demons started coming out of this woman, who the students were praying for in her hut. The next day, they continued the work, praying for her and commanding the demons to release her. The students would command the demons to identify themselves as they came out, and the names were recorded. Often, the woman would tell them that they were leaving. By Thursday, 260 demons had been cast out of her.

Often the demons would protest about having to leave. But they always did, especially when the students sang songs about the blood of Jesus. They hated, in particular, the hymn "There is a Fountain Filled with Blood."

Mbangiye, the elephant-hunter-turned-pastor, was the one recording the names of the spirits. Some were named after sins: Bitterness, anger, greed. Some were ancestral names, or the names associated with the ancestor worship and animism common in the area, which the demons would use, purporting to be one of the people's ancestors.

Gordon asked what had started this problem. It turned out the husband's family hated the woman for not having more children. She had only one. They wanted to get rid of her, and she had grown very bitter in response to many of their insults. Some were among the worst: someone had urinated on one of her belongings. Someone had also left excrement on the trail to her outhouse.

Her bitterness had apparently opened the door for a whole hierarchy of demons to attack her.

On the first night of ministry to this person, Geneva was taking turns sitting with two teen-age girls who had been delivered, memorizing scriptures to redirect their minds.

She finally went to bed late, very tired, while Gordon and the students were still casting out demons from the wife of the choir director. She was staying in the pastor's hut with one of the girls who still had demons. This girl would get upset and go into a fit anytime any other person already affected by demons would come near her. To help her get rest, Geneva was staying with her.

Suddenly Geneva was awakened by a huge noise. It was the sound of a stampede outside her hut, and her first thought was that a thundering giant herd of goats was running through the village. But there was no herd like that at the village.

It made no sense, yet she knew she was fully awake and not dreaming. She thought something must have scared some herd that she never would have imagined was anywhere near.

Suddenly it was over. And she knew there was something strange, not right about it. Then she sensed that what she had heard was demons leaving that village.

The men had not cast out many that first night, Monday, but who could know how many demons had been waiting there to take over the whole place, Geneva asks. "We knew it was a crucial time, a war situation between the two clans."

When Gordon came home to the pastor's house, he crawled in through a window so he would not disturb the girl sleeping in the hut.

Gordon had barely laid down when a girl across the path started going wild. Several of the students were trying to cast demons out of her, but they were not having any results. Geneva told Gordon he'd better go see about it, and he did, going back out through the window.

He took her to the church, and he and the students worked with her. A demon came out of her. That brief instance was one of the five deliverances of the week, and it was the easiest.

The next day, Gordon and the students went back to work with the wife of the choir director. They had accounted for 260 demons leaving this girl, but she still had symptoms of a problem. There was a holdout.

The woman could tell them that not all the spirits were gone. While some of these demons had sometimes driven this woman totally out of control and out of her mind, this one had apparently receded, trying to stay in the background and keep its place.

The ministry to this woman went on all day. There seemed to be no results at all. But the woman insisted he was there.

By 10:30 that night, the scene had gotten eerie and grotesque. They had no candles, and the dark hut was being lit by curved pieces of broken pottery containing some palm oil and a bit of burning cloth. It created an oily, smoky light that cast weird shadows in the hut.

Gordon had been commanding this demon — "Who are you? come out!" — for what seemed endless hours. That night, the demon finally admitted he was there, he was the chief of the possessing spirits, and he would not come out. All this time, it took two men to hold the girl down. The students would work in shifts just to restrain her.

Gordon was becoming exasperated. He was wondering if this entity would ever come out, but he never let on. Gordon prayed, 'Lord, what should we do?' and the answer came to him clearly:

Sing.

What do we sing?

Up from the Grave He Arose.

Gordon and the others turned in their Lingala hymnals and began to sing:

> *Low in the grave he lay, Jesus my Savior!*
> *Waiting the coming day, Jesus my Lord!*
> *Up from the grave He arose,*
> *With a mighty triumph o'er his foes;*
> *He arose a victor from the dark domain,*
> *And he lives forever with his saints to reign,*
> *He arose! He arose! Hallelujah, Christ arose!*

"When we got to the chorus, 'Up from the grave He arose,' it was like heaven opened," Gordon says. "The demon had no more power in view of the resurrection. We were on our feet, praising the Lord. The devil was screaming and said his name, Gbandakula. Then the woman fell over. She seemed dead."

The devil's name (pronounced Bann-da-koo-la) was also that of one of the most powerful witch doctors who had ever lived in the area. Some of the people, including the pastor, Mbangiye, put their hands over their mouths in shock when they heard the name. There is no question in Gordon's mind that he had been confronting the evil spirit that had empowered the dreaded witch doctor who had died years ago.

It was over. The woman came to with a smile on her face and asked them to sing again.

"We sang for a while and encouraged them to memorize verses, because the devil will try to come back," Gordon says. "About midnight, the woman was with her husband, the choir director. All of these people were exhausted. The demons came back, probably the Gbandakula, and went after the husband's soul. ... When they came, they said it was like a big hand went *pow!* against the house. It could have crumbled it. Then they attacked him. But she commanded them to get out of there, and they left. It was a great victory for her, too."

Gordon feels that with the departure of Gbandakula, the entire group of demons left, too. The difference in the village was noticeable. The next morning as he walked through the village, people were all smiles, and there was a peace.

The next Sunday was Easter. Geneva realized that this village had just experienced the power of the resurrection.

"In the midst of that week of deliverance, I had been walking at night toward the hut where we stayed, and it struck me that I should feel eerie and scared," Geneva says. "Instead, I had the greatest sense of peace you can imagine. It was something to really experience how God's power is so much greater than all these other powers."

"It was an experience that really made us realize there is nothing God cannot do," Gordon says. "Nothing. Even get 261 demons out of a woman, one of those demons the strongest.

"And we come home to the states and wonder 'What's their problem?' They talk about finances. Oh? What's new? The church has financial problems? Ah, well. Minor."

It wasn't long, however, before Gordon and Geneva felt the devil was trying to strike back. Gordon tells the story:

"It was a beautiful, sunny Saturday morning at the Bible Institute in Goyongo. Geneva and I were headed for Karawa on the first leg of our flight home for our son Michael's wedding. We were four passengers, no, five, for the other lady passenger was heading for Karawa for the delivery of her first child.

"After takeoff and four minutes into the flight, I asked the pilot, Steve Adams, 'How goes your day?' He replied nonchalantly, 'Real good!'

"Just then, the airplane motor stopped. Unbeknown to us, a 2-inch piece of metal, vital to the flow of gas to the motor, just then suffered metal fatigue and broke. All of Steve's frantic activity was counterproductive. We quickly lost altitude to the extent that it was impossible to turn around and land at the Goyongo airstrip.

"Steve sent a 'Mayday ' message as the plane dropped toward the jungle. 'Charlie Mike Uniform going down!'

"We literally cried out to the Lord. God had mercy on all six of us. We skimmed the top of giant jungle trees as Steve tried to reach a small plateau filled with very tall elephant grass.

"Geneva, from her side of the plane, saw a huge tree limb that looked like it would tear off the left wing in our descent. Miraculously, we passed that hurdle and felt our wheels come down on the solid ground. Solid, that is, except for the ant hills popping under the weight and force of the plane.

"One ant hill was too solid for even a plane hurtling along the ground. The strut on the left side buckled, and the plane stopped in a lopsided position with the gas from the left wing pouring out of the overflow vent. 'Everybody out!' shouted Steve.

"I looked back and realized that Steve and I were the only ones left in the plane. We hurriedly ran back to an open place and thanked God for His deliverance.

"I called as loudly as possible, and finally heard a reply from a village hunter. He was a stutterer. When he saw the downed plane and missionaries standing near it, his only question was, 'Di-di-did you sur-sur-survive?'

"He took a written note to the missionaries at Goyongo. Our 'Mayday' also had been intercepted, so help was on the way, and word of our crash was passed around the 11:30 a.m. network.

"They found us about two or three hours later and escorted us down the hill to safety and a good night of rest at Goyongo.

"The Christensens' names were up for prayer that day in the Covenant Church's Missionary Prayer Booklet! What a great answer to many prayers for our protection and deliverance!"

Life Lessons

The term 1974-77 was very hard on the Christensen family. Not only was the family separated, with Michael and Susan attending school in the U.S., but Gordon and Geneva had entered an area of ministry that must be entered carefully.

It was this term that they learned the hard way an invaluable lesson for all parents: Pray diligently for your children.

"When you are in ministry, where the devil is after you at every crook in the road, if he can't get you, he will try to get your children," Geneva says.

This term of spiritual warfare, however, they realized they had to do more than pray for their children. They had to do warfare praying for them. A satanic attack on one of their children showed them that "those kids have to be covered constantly by the blood of the Lord Jesus Christ," Geneva says. "It was a very difficult experience, but we, including our children, also saw the power of the Lord to overcome. That does not mean you simply say, 'Lord, overcome this for me,' and it happens in the blink of an eye. Because for us, it has not. It has been really warfare praying, and sometimes for a considerable time."

"The basic facts are that we were in spiritual warfare in Wasolo and teaching the demonology class in Goyongo," Gordon says. "As a consequence, we knew the basic plan of covering ourselves and daily putting on the armor of God. Of course, our children had not had this experience."

"This really opened my eyes to how wicked the devil is," Geneva says. "He will attack not only adults, but children, babies. Anybody. That's where we as parents need to protect our children. Particularly when we are in these areas of work.

"This is a teaching that most missionaries never think of; we didn't think of it in our early years — the devil attacking our children. As I look back, I think some of the sickness was to get us discouraged and everything, if not through ourselves, then through our children. This one experience (with one of the children) really opened our eyes."

Geneva mentions the book *The Adversary*, written by Pastor Martin Bubeck and published by Moody Press. Pastor Bubeck was thrown into the deliverance ministry much as Pastor Fred Neth had been at Midway Covenant Church. However, Bubeck, a Baptist minister, wrote of an attack of satanic oppression on his daughter. Her rescue changed the direction of his ministry and ultimately the establishment of a clinic in Souix City, Iowa, that is staffed by medical doctors, psychologists, psychiatrists and pastors who are able to wage spiritual warfare.

However, Bubeck's experience as well as their own has moved prayer for their children to the forefront of their prayer lives, Gordon and Geneva say. Children are usually unprepared for warfare praying or the concepts of "putting on the whole armor of God" that the Apostle Paul wrote about in the book of Ephesians. Nor are many Christian adults for that matter, Gordon says, although he thinks that is changing.

"I think this is one of the big differences that will happen to Christians from this point on," he says.

And perhaps just in the nick of time, the Christensens feel. The conduct of youths in the U.S., which is reinforced in popular entertainment, indicate to Gordon and Geneva that our youth are very much under attack by spiritual evil.

Of the girls they delivered that week described above, three of the five were teens (however, Gordon and Geneva had many deliverance experiences with all ages of people, both men and women). One of their first responses to deliverance prayers was a very cynical, cocky, impertinent attitude. But in short order much more pronounced manifestations would begin, assuring Gordon and Geneva that they were dealing with more than a kid who didn't want to be prayed for.

"You see that in a lot of teens here," Gordon says of the attitude he came to recognize as a signal. "That really bothered me. I thought, 'Man alive, we are just on the fringe. These kids here at home are on the fringe of allowing a demonic power to enter into that kind of an attitude.

"When we see kids here who are impolite, caustic, insolently wearing ball caps in prayer meetings, all we can think is, 'Are these the initial stages by which the devil eventually intends to take over their lives?' Because we saw that insolence in these teenagers who were demon possessed, and it didn't look much different."

A look at the daily news in the 1990s, however, shows an "insolence" being taken to horrible new heights by more and more youths in the U.S. A popular Christian song talks about how the conduct problems of the 1940s involved chewing gum or talking in class. Fifty years later, rapes and killings occur at schools, administrators consider electronic scanners at school doors to counter the problem of students carrying weapons, and classroom corridors are patrolled by police officers.

"You wonder, where is the cutoff line?" Geneva asks. "Some of them, through their behavior, go on even to suicide. The statistics are terribly high. This I don't doubt, because so many young people open themselves wide to demonic powers. The music, the TV they listen to, the Ouija board, drugs, all kinds of things."

The Christensens are sure that demons can find entry into a life by something as easily overlooked as an attitude.

"That's the way," Gordon says. "I think there is no question about it. The trail of disobedience, when it is full blown — if you go back to see it start, it may be such a simple thing as a child saying, 'I am not going to do it.'

"When parents see an attitude developing in their kids that is foreign to them, strange, that could be an attack that the enemy is using to get them to squirm out of parental authority and into disobedience, to isolate themselves from normal channels of control over them that God intended. God intended that there be control."

To Gordon, the working of disobedience in a youth toward a parent or teacher is intended to result in something much deeper: ultimately, defiance and disobedience to God.

They offer some practical tips on spiritual warfare:
- A good marital relationship is vital. The first epistle of Peter teaches that strife in that relationship will actually hinder prayers. Husband and wife must "get their acts together," with special emphasis on togetherness. They are considered "one flesh," or a single entity, in God's eyes, and must be in sync to succeed. This is why Gordon and Geneva did so much work on the home life of Africans during their missionary years.

- Parent-child relationships are vital. One of the biggest warnings of the Bible to fathers in particular is being so heavy-handed with authority that it engenders bitterness in a child, a key avenue for demons.

"So many people were shocked that you would ever ask your child to forgive you for something you might have done," Gordon says. "They could never conceive of bowing to a child and admitting they were less than perfect. ... A total misunderstanding of meekness. They thought meekness was weakness. I talked to pastors, lay preachers and Bible Institute grads on this very thing — if your child is going into teen years, or is in teen years and is rebelling, then very likely you have said or done something that has embittered that child. ... What you need to do is sit them down alone and ask them, Have I done anything that has caused to you to be bitter toward me?'"

Gordon tells of one father who took the advice with his eldest daughter, who had been saddled with much of the child-rearing of brothers and sisters and home duties when the mother was not around. The father had also had a bad but common habit of ordering her around like a servant, to get him a drink or do some errand. He also had a ready insult if she wasn't quick to respond to his instructions: "What's the matter? Have you lost your ears?"

Such words angered her, and it grew into bitterness.

But when the father asked her about her anger toward him, she showed him her point of view — and he apologized for the way he had treated her. "I didn't realize I was hurting you so deeply," he said. And he changed.

"It was probably one of the finest things he did in child-rearing," Gordon says. "If that daughter had persisted in that bitterness, there was a likelihood she would have been molested by a demon, because they are looking for an opportunity."

- Pray the same way for others. "The devil wants us confused and unable to focus on what we are doing," Gordon says. "So also pray for those who might, by having a problem, distract you from your target."
- Persevere. "You often must just faithfully go about doing what the Lord has called you to do, even if you may never have the privilege of seeing the fruit," Geneva says. "That is really not our privilege ... it may be years down the road and is up to the Lord. ... But we must persevere in what God is opening up to us today. It may take a lot of watering by other people, or perhaps I am watering today what someone else has planted. It is a cooperative thing. I think we have to keep this in mind, that we don't start thinking, 'This is my segment, and I am going to see it in.' Because we can start growing in the essence of pride, that 'I did this project' and 'I accomplished this,' and that is exactly what the Lord doesn't want to happen."
- Value the scriptures, and invest in them. "My real knowledge of the scriptures dates from the time I started teaching at the Bible Institute," Gordon says. "I went to seminary, but somehow seminaries have a tremendous facility for teaching around the Word, but not the Word."

For Geneva, the door to scriptures opened by seeking answers in the Bible to the problems women brought to her. She wanted women to read the Bible themselves, and in so doing she read with them and learned greatly.

For children, memorizing scriptures is a key to them "Putting on the whole armor of God" they are going to need in life.

- Remember that we've won the war. "The sequel of the story about the woman who was delivered (from 261 demons) is that she and her husband went off to junior Bible school and became the local Bible school pastors in their village, and as far as I know are still ministering," Gordon says. "I remember talking to her one time: 'How are you doing?' No problem. She had learned her defenses. Probably sings 'There is a Fountain Filled with Blood'!

"Demons hate anything that tells about the victory of the cross," he continues. "And, of course, that is exactly what the cross is. It is a victory over the world, the flesh and the devil. Our trinity of enemies was conquered at the cross. So when you talk about the cross, you talk about total victory, and the devils know it better than we do."

Chapter 17

The Most Valuable Harvest

It was night as Geneva looked out the window at her family's farm, and a full, bright moon rose in the east to illuminate it in pale light.

Geneva's father had died a month earlier, in May 1975, and she had come home to be with her family and help her mother move off this farm to town.

With the moon for light, she could see the land where she had grown up. She stood in the tiny house where she had been born and her mother had spent her entire married life. Nearby was the creek where the family would go fishing with their dad after a hard day's work. There was the pasture where the neighbor kids came for Sunday baseball, and the fence she had learned to follow home from school if a dust storm suddenly struck.

Geneva's brother, Ed, and his wife, Ruth, had been home on furlough when Dave Noren died at age 85. Her son, Michael, had just returned from Zaire, where he was a short termer for a year, and was now attending Le Tourneau Technical Institute in Longview, Texas. Michael had gotten home just in time to attend the funeral. But Geneva could not get back in time. Now she was there to help and to say her goodbyes.

The scene before her on that June night brought back a flood of childhood memories of the many good times the Norens had had growing up in some of the hardest years of the century. And she could see how, though probably the poorest farm in the area, it was a place where God had been been working in them all.

She remembered how her dad loved to collect Indian arrowheads in a couple of the fields. He had studied Indian lore and loved to tell the children stories about the people who had lived on this land before them. Dave Noren had always been sympathetic for minority groups and underdogs and had spent a lot of time learning about Native Americans. That concern for others had clearly been passed on to his children.

She remembered the tiny house being full of music. Her mother would play an organ that a neighbor had loaned them, and Dave would play a violin and other instruments with skill he had developed on his own.

The house had been full of fun. The kids would play ping pong on the dining room table.

All these memories were being built in the midst of a severe poverty that weighed on Dave much more heavily than Geneva realized until she was older. His family lived from hand to mouth for years, and worry often had Dave pacing the barn floor long into the night. Geneva learned .later that Dad's thoughts on those long stretches were about how the family was going to make it.

Yet as she looked over the homestead that night, she realized she couldn't have been born at a better place or time, or to better parents, in order to get ready for the course her life would take. In a sense, this had been a training camp, and God had been there all along, even if others might have wondered.

When Geneva went for nurses' training at Swedish Covenant Hospital in Chicago, and then to North Park, she realized how poor they had been. She also sensed a stigma for being from the Dust Bowl. Some people seemed to think that those who lived there were responsible for the event. She saw how the kids she was with couldn't understand the poverty.

During a visit home in her adulthood, her father was very apologetic for that poverty.

"He said, 'I wish we had adequate funds when you were little so we could have given you things that the other children had. So we could have helped with your education,'" Geneva recalls. "Well, none of us lacked education through lack of funds. ... And we learned some very good lessons in our home because we were totally dependent on God. ... We learned that God was real. He was not something you go to on Sunday at a church service. We couldn't go to church every week, because we didn't have the gas. But God was real to us all through the week. I think I learned early on that God is a real, real person. Happiness does not depend on material things, but on relations and family stability."

A lot of lifetime lessons had been taught on that farm, but the time for those lessons had passed. So on that June night, there was a sense of goodbye in the sweet country air. The training camp for the Norens was closing. Esther Amanda Noren would be moving into Oberlin the next day, and though the farm would remain in Willard's control, this homestead would lose its position as the family center, the anchor, the "home" that was out there for Gordon and Geneva's children as they grew up in Africa. With Dave and Amanda there, it had been the safe harbor that everyone could always visit and stay near.

As Geneva looked out the window at that moonlit farm, another lesson was being underscored in her heart: This had also been the stage on which a cast of characters valued by God, and each other, had been developed.

Geneva could see those characters, and the character they built in the children, going back generations. One of the treasures she inherited from her grandmother, for example, was the oft-repeated saying, "It can be did." The lesson stuck for generations.

"Nothing is impossible with the Lord," Geneva says. "It came from grandma, to her daughter and on to us."

One of the other principles in the operation of that little farm was individual responsibility. Dave Noren was particularly emphatic on that point.

"We had to accept responsibility for our behavior," Geneva says. "We had to take responsibility for what happened. If we broke a glass washing dishes, we didn't say, 'it fell.' It was, "I dropped it.' Sometimes I think that was a little too severe, but I also think that is one of the big lacks in today's society. You can excuse anything if you look far enough."

Coupled with the emphasis on personal accountability was also the responsibility for forgiveness.

"Our parents wouldn't let us do anything else until we asked forgiveness if we did something to another. We didn't always want to do it, but we had to do it, and it is amazing how it does repair the breach, and then we could go on playing. An important lesson to remember for all the days of our lives."

Those were the kinds of things Geneva was taking away from the farm. From the window where she stood, it looked a lot like many other farms in Decatur County, Kansas, and probably a little less than them. It would never be the same family farm again. But the fruit that had been borne on it over the seasons had ended up touching the world, feeding many in this land and others, just as a few simple loaves and fishes in the hands of the Lord had benefited a multitude.

A rich legacy had grown from humble ground, proving the truth of Grandma Carlson's favorite saying.

Life Lessons

- God is no respecter of persons. That is a well-known saying, but people often overlook the truth of it because the world is so much a respecter of persons. From caste systems to Hollywood celebrity status, the societies of the world are geared to value some people more than others. That is not God's doing, but people's.

Geneva saw God's viewpoint so clearly on the mission field. She was often in the presence of renowned missionaries, and she says she would think, 'Who am I, from a corn patch in Kansas, to be with these persons?'

"It doesn't matter where you're born, it doesn't matter what kind of house you grew up in, if you are willing to give yourself to the Lord. God is real, is faithful and answers prayer."

- Start discipline when children are young. Geneva learned from her own experiences on the farm that good parental discipline is the key to self-discipline, which is the precursor to Godly discipline, or obedience to God.

- Be consistent with children. The Bible speaks of God's consistency with his children, even though the world they live in will not be consistent. A solid pattern in relationship is a foundation on which children can build, rather than the day-to-day living conditions they face, which can shift like sand.

- Children need to know the adults are in charge, and children need them to be. Likewise, adults need to know that God expects them to use that authority wisely. God "raises the bar" on authorities; with expanded authority comes expanded responsibility. Jesus said:

...*For unto whomsoever much is given, of him shall be much required.* — Luke 12:48

With knowledge, with adulthood, with independence comes accountability for how they are used.

- A child's selfishness must be broken, but not his spirit.

Selfishness can do the damage of an earthquake, and yet it is common to man. The Bible is replete with messages and warnings about selfishness and how easily it is turned against us. because it will keep us from following God wholeheartedly. Yet unwise parenting can do a lot of damage in the name of good intentions. So there is a tightrope to walk. Paul wrote:

> *Fathers, provoke not your children to anger, lest they be discouraged.* — Colossians 3:21

- "It can be did." Nothing is impossible with the Lord.

Chapter 18

Committing Truths To Paper

After three decades serving in Africa at schools, hospitals, mission stations and villages, Gordon and Geneva turned their emphasis to writing Christian materials. They had already written a series of tracts and booklets on family and Christian living issues. Now they were launching a major writing project: the first Bible commentary on the New Testament ever written in Lingala.

Though the last term had seen a lot of spiritual warfare, their term had been structured around block teaching, or three-month stints at Wasolo, Bokada, Bumba and the Bible Institute. With their main duty as teachers, they had continued to expand their scope of the Bible.

In 1980 and '81, Gordon and Geneva were established fulltime in a house in Bokada, where they worked almost exclusively on the first of a three-volume commentary. In 1982-83, they returned to Salina, Kansas, where they spent the year doing the final preparations for printing. The first volume was published in 1983 by Graphics Church Press in Glendale, Calif. In 1984, they were back in Africa, where they began work on the second volume. It proved to be another very challenging year.

The trouble began while Geneva was teaching at a women's conference.

"I was in a hut with a woman, they brought us some food and I turned around to my trunk to get a spoon," Geneva says. "When I turned, something happened to my back and I was in excruciating pain. I was speaking, doing the Bible teaching at the camp that week, and it was horrible. I could hardly get off my camp cot and get over, and I'd hang onto the pulpit. The pain was excruciating. The Africans wanted to send into the station to get them to come and get me, but I said 'No, we're going to finish this conference.'"

She did manage through the week, and little by little over the months, her back got better. On a trip several months later to another conference, the truck Gordon was driving got stuck in a deep hole, and the passengers were trying to pry it out with long poles. Geneva was helping when she felt a searing pain in her back.

She managed for several more months, which included a one-month teaching trip to Bozogi, about 80 kilometers from Bumba, where they were stationed that year. The only way she could ease the pain was to lie across her camp cot on her knees or lie down flat.

"I was praying, 'Lord, help us get back to Bumba somehow.' The pain was indescribable. 'Lord, you could take this pain away for a day.' The roads were so bad, I knew we were going to get stuck."

On the day they were leaving Bozogi, she remembers looking at the cab of the truck and wondering, "How will I get in there?"

"Then a woman saw my predicament, and before I knew it, she had picked me up and set me in the seat!" Geneva was stunned. The woman's strength, built from years of carrying heavy loads, enabled her to lift Geneva almost shoulder height and set her down as lightly as a feather. Her problem was solved. Geneva thanked the woman who had been used to answer her prayer.

But the ride was still a bouncing back-breaker for Geneva. Each rut was agonizing. Finally, the problem Geneva had been worrying about for weeks was before her. A section of road was so bad that the group could count on getting stuck.

"The road was gone, but there was a ridge that you would try to hang onto until you slipped in, then you had to dig your way out," Geneva says.

She and their two African companions got out and walked across the ridge, then the Africans rolled up their pants legs, getting ready to wade into the muddy hole and help Gordon out.

"All of a sudden, he was coming across on this ridge, and there wasn't enough room for four wheels," Geneva says. "Two wheels had slipped down on the side of this hole, and two wheels were up in the air! He was barreling across there on two wheels! The Africans stood there, and I did too, and I thought, 'I have never seen anything like this in my life!'

"He didn't go down in the hole. He came across on two wheels in that big old truck and plopped down on the other side. I thought, 'Lord, you didn't take away my pain, but you did shorten our trip.' We got in, thanked the Lord and went."

However, even with doctors' care and traction, Geneva kept getting worse. The pain of traction was so terrible that she sent word to the hospital at Karawa that she couldn't tolerate it. She was told she needed to be at the Karawa hospital, so an MAF pilot laid the seat of his plane back, loaded her in and flew her there.

"There just so happened to be a neurosurgeon, of all things, visiting at the time," Geneva says. "We don't have neurosurgeons passing through that often."

"He said, 'It's evident what your problem is. You have at least one disk that is out.' My legs were starting to go then, which was really frightening. He said, 'You have to go home and have surgery, but it will go fine, and you'll be back in a short time."

For Geneva, it was yet another frustrating setback. They had just gotten back and had not even fulfilled a year. The doctor's advice was very discouraging.

The Covenant and Free Church maintained a radio network and sometimes would have prayer over it through the night. That night missionaries across the Free Church and Covenant fields prayed for her in hour or half-hour segments until the sun came up.

"That night, I slept," Geneva says. "In the morning my leg felt so much better. I could lift it off the bed. I still didn't know why I'd had a good night, and they told me the people had been praying all night. Then I said to Dr. Rog (Roger Thorpe, who had worked on their field many years) 'Now I can stay. I can lift my leg a little bit.' He said, 'No, you go home while you can lift your leg.'

"I thought it was such a tragedy to end up our first year on the field like this. The expense. Just starting down there in Bumba. We were to have a young couple coming soon to work with us. Then we had to go home."

When Geneva arrived in Chicago, she had lost a good deal of the use of both legs. She was immediately admitted to Swedish Covenant Hospital. The next morning, Gordon had an office at the denomination's headquarters, where he could concentrate on writing the manuscript of a Lingala commentary.

The Christensens were in the U.S. from December 1984 to August 1985. Gordon completed the manuscript, and while Geneva was recuperating from back surgery, she proofread.

Her doctor in the states did not want Geneva going back to Africa that fall, but he approved after he got her to promise not to ride in a truck for a year.

She returned to the city of Bumba and kept her promise, traveling by plane and riverboat back to the immense, old Belgian house where they had been staying. The typewriters resumed their clacking while both Gordon and Geneva also continued teaching courses. Geneva could walk to five teaching sites from her home and also supervised "Emmaus" classes by correspondence. In 1987, they finished Volume

Three of the commentary, the first complete New Testament commentary in Lingala.

LIFE LESSONS

They saw many disappointments and distractions but saw success as well. What would look like delays in their agenda would still prove useful.

Chapter 19

Watching the Spirit Move

Returning to the United States in 1987, Gordon and Geneva first stayed in an interdenominational housing complex for missionaries in New Jersey until they decided they would make Florida their retirement home — or home base. Though they bought a doublewide mobile home in a village in Oldsmar, they were a long way from settling down.

First, their official retirement would not come until 1990. Second, Gordon and Geneva don't seem to believe in retirement anyway.

In those closing years, they found themselves being asked to be guest speakers at retreats and at churches. Within nine months, they had itinerated at 13 churches across the United States.

As they were teaching, they were also observing. And Gordon and Geneva saw much that concerned them. Among their observations:

- It seemed that almost every Christian family they met was in some sort of crisis, especially with the children. Often these were adult children, going through divorce or other hardship. Also, disturbingly, often the people hurting the most were in church leadership. Geneva said she soon found that her ministry seemed to be one-on-one with the wives of ministers.

"I guess the thing that bothered me a lot was, what had happened to the power of the Word of God in these kids' lives?" Geneva says.

- The church was in an era of not wanting to be different from the world. "There seems there was breakdown of the Christians' willingness to say, 'I will be different from the world because Christ is dwelling in me,'" Geneva says.
- The church had forgotten "God's mathematics," as Gordon calls it. The rule: the key to increase is giving.

"I hear all kinds of things like, 'How are we going to keep our pastor?' No! Give him away. God never intended you to keep your pastor, or these people. The more we try to keep, the fewer, the less, we get. It's true of everything. Divide and multiply. We bring our schemes for economic success into the church and say, 'It worked out there, it will work here.'

"We copied, we emulated — we telemarketed. Is that really what God wanted? We were reading this morning in Acts Chapter 9. Peter goes to Sharon and Lydda, heals one person and both towns turn to God en masse. Well, that was the way God did it. I think that may be the final observation: Rediscover God's way of doing it.

"I was asking the Lord the other day, 'What do you want?' And clear as a bell, the Lord said, 'I don't want a performance. I want worship.' Our services are never meant to be a performance, but worship. And of course, when you have that, you have revival."

- The church wanted security and predictability. As a culture, we want organized backup systems, "Plan Bs" and guarantees, from our elaborate medical care system to guarantees of a good retirement. To us, help should never be farther than a cellular phone call away.

The result has been an assumption that we provide for ourselves, and we don't truly look to God for provision, say Gordon and Geneva. But insisting on guarantees in life means staying in bondage in Egypt, not venturing into the desert. The Christensens have come to believe that to depend on our own strength and plans is to give up on our abilities through God's Kingdom as well as our greatest position of influence in the world.

- The church coveted comfort and ownership. This has had the church "boxed in" spiritually, Gordon says. Pastors constantly bump against this desire by the congregation to "domesticate" him or her, although the search committee said it wanted a leader. What they meant was, they want someone to run the shop. "They do not want a leader, someone entrepreneurial who will rock the boat, make waves. They want somebody who will do maintenance. That is what I thought was happening."

- We are very slow to respond. That is in part, Gordon says, because we have so much and are so comfortable. In essence, each American citizen has thousands serving him, from getting him mail on time, his paper delivered and immediate emergency care to making sure the trash is gone before it smells too bad. In contrast, much of the world, including Zaire, lives with sewage in the streets and sometimes garbage piles so high on city curbs (as they saw once in Kinshasa) that a driver can't see the storefronts. Our comfort makes us lethargic and complacent.

- Something was stirring. A spiritual need was being felt in America's churches. "Now I know what it was," Gordon says. "I think we are in the midst of a worldwide prayer movement, and we were seeing little beginnings way back then."

- Americans were becoming less self-conscious and more God-conscious in such things as form in church. There was more emotion, clapping, crying, heart-felt praise than in the formal settings that once dominated Sunday mornings. "A marvelous answer to prayer," says Gordon.

But their travels to Africa were not over yet. After nine months of itinerating in the U.S., and with about a year to go before retirement, Gordon and Geneva were asked by the Home Board and the African church to go to the capital city of Kinshasa to help their daughter Mary and her husband, Dennis, get started as missionaries in Zaire. The young couple had been asked to serve there by the African Church Council and Home Board. However, the Covenant Church had said it needed some veterans to help them get established. Gordon and Geneva said they would be glad to help. They locked up their mobile home and were off again.

Kinshasa was a huge city with problems like any other major metropolitan area, if not more pronounced. About 2 percent of the population was very wealthy, and the rest were in abject poverty. A middle class was nearly nonexistent.

Gordon and Geneva arrived about six months before Dennis and Mary. In that time they found a house, a car and started making contacts with the people. When Dennis and Mary arrived in July 1990, they could get straight to work. Gordon and Geneva stayed on about a year and a half to help.

"The idea was to plant churches," Gordon says. When they arrived, the Covenant Mission had one church in a heavily populated area of Kinshasa. They eventually established two more.

"The first thing we did was get a piece of land. In this one place, we put up a little structure, about 10 by 20, and then we would go marching through the area (led by a four-piece band) inviting people. In the other place, we just had a few bricks and rocks, and we put them in a circle and invited people to come sit on a brick. We started out with kids. Then the kids brought their parents."

Most of the people in Kinshasa had some familiarity with Christianity but were not converted, Gordon says. And life was harder. One reason: the people had less independence than their rural brothers and sisters, because they did not have a garden — a food supply. A second reason: people were usually desperately poor and ready to do what it took to get by.

"The city social problems seemed harder to deal with," Geneva says. "It is a lot like here; you can be in church on Sunday and be anonymous the rest of the week. There was a lot of unfaithfulness, even in so-called Christian families. Very difficult things.

"One woman wanted to stay and pray after a service. She was being given a house to live in in return for her marital services. So if she cut off this relationship, she wouldn't have a house to live in. That was the kind of thing we had to deal with. There was a lot of this to have to deal with in the Kinshasa churches."

This was not unheard of upcountry. But it was not condoned by the church and was dealt with by the elders.

"In Kinshasa, it was so interwoven into their lives and existence that it was extremely difficult," Geneva says. "They lived with an unclear conscience, knowing they were living in sin."

Gordon and Geneva knew God could provide for the people, and would. That is how they had lived their own lives.

"But some are not willing to take that step," Geneva says. In the case of the one woman who asked for prayer, the man who was keeping her provided nice clothes, housing, "and she didn't want to step down from that. It was a matter of choice."

Teetering from social instability, Kinshasa finally tumbled into chaos in the summer of 1991 when the army could not be paid. Gordon and Geneva had finished their year's assistance in September and left without incident. But the signs of trouble were evident as they flew out of Kinshasa in September. Dennis and Mary were ordered to evacuate shortly afterward.

Gordon and Geneva were official retirees. Their final day had occurred earlier in the year, on Gordon's birthday, but they had stayed on extra months to help Dennis and Mary.

They left knowing that even after 40 years in Africa, there was still a lot of work to do. And they could see that for Dennis and Mary, the journey of missionary life was going to be about as smooth as theirs had been.

The only hope was to put it in God's hands.

LIFE LESSONS

Gordon and Geneva have seen over the years that they must do their part and let God do His part of any project. And the more they have respected this, the easier the work has become. Jesus told those who would take his yoke upon them would find the burden is light, and the Christensens have learned that He knew what He was talking about.

"So much of what we were doing was really just observing what God was doing," Gordon says. "It was such a privilege to see."

One example was a 10-day trip to Wapinda, a remote area, in 1951. There seemed to be no results to that trip at the time.

About 25 years later, they were invited to a church dedication in a very remote area that they could not even recall visiting.

"We got to this place, got out of the pickup, and the people gathered around us," Geneva says. "Now they were going to have a Big Sunday, which meant this was a central district with a good-sized church. And they looked at us and said, 'You know, we have seen you before. You were here years ago.'"

Geneva figured they were thinking of Jody LaVahn, who worked at Wasolo many years, but they said no, they knew Jody. "You were here many years ago with a little baby."

They went on and described their entire visit. "This weekend we are dedicating a church on the site where the house was you stayed in."

Gordon and Geneva asked them, "Was there any fruit of our coming that time?"

One man in the group told them yes, that after they had left, 12 to 15 got together and started praying and asking God to send a teacher to their area. Then they walked for miles to a place closer to Wasolo and asked Art Lunblad if they could have a preacher come to them. Little by little, they got a preacher over there. "And this is the result," the man said.

"You know," Gordon says, "It was a thrill to see what the Lord would do, and totally hidden from our eyes for all that

The first baptism at Kinkole, 1991, one of the Kinshasa churches.

time. We never had any idea how the Lord had used that. .... That gave us a lot of encouragement, because sometimes you feel like you're beating your body to the hilt, and you don't have any strength left, and you don't see a thing happen. But that was one time He let us have a little peek at what He'd done."

A return visit in 1996 to their Tandala home from 1953-57, with Mary Lynn and her children.

Chapter 20

Just Saying No To Rocking Chairs

Their "retirement" in Florida would be more accurately described as a transfer to a new mission field. For Gordon and Geneva, "missionary" is a state of being, not a career. They are involved in a Covenant Church in Clearwater, and they spend a lot of time on the road.

At the request of the Covenant denomination, Gordon and Geneva have served as instructors in the "School of Prayer and Evangelism" seminars held at churches across the country. Gordon has been invited to speak to a seminary class at North Park and to individual churches, including an infant church in the former Yugoslavia. The couple has served as interim pastors and, more than once during the course of interviews for their biography, stopped to offer long-distance counsel to people across the country who called for help or advice.

During those years after official retirement in 1991, they'd been back twice, serving as guest speakers at the churches in Zaire.

However, they've found that the greatest rewards are in seeing doors to witness open through friendships they have made close to home. They say the mission field is where you are.

At home in their retirement community, Gordon and Geneva have seen the comfortably retired struggling just as much with the issues of life as any African ever did. Often in the U.S., it is for purpose. After years of working to get to retirement, many find there's little to it except going to a different restaurant for supper and, as is the case in their part of Florida, risking hard-earned retirement savings on casino ships that sail daily into the Gulf of Mexico.

But the Christensens are finding that in their retirement, God still opens doors for them to serve Him better.

"One of the great things about retirement is not having any timetable but the Lord's," Gordon says.

It has allowed him, for example, to be checking on a bill at a hospital when a man Gordon and Geneva had been praying for walks out of the emergency room. His wife was there. The man saw Gordon, grabbed him and took him back in to pray with him and her.

There was also a close friend in the neighborhood who, through God's grace, Gordon and Geneva could be with at his greatest hour of need.

The story began when the friend, Bill, came to their door saying he thought his wife had had a stroke. He was right, and Geneva helped get her to the emergency room and stayed with her, even to her dying moments.

It was a time when her experience would be tapped again. She spoke the Word to her friend, Pat.

"I think it's important to be speaking the Word to someone who is passing on from this world to the next," Geneva says. Not only because of the comfort it can bring, but she has learned from experience that even in these final moments, the devil does not quit.

She learned this lesson in part through the death of a missionary she had worked with in Zaire. This woman's daughter had told Geneva that before the woman's death in the U.S., she had suddenly rallied the last of her strength to shout in Lingala at an unseen intruder, "You get out of my house! You have no place to be in here, because I am the Lord's!"

What powerful, valuable last words! They exposed the enemy once again and showed to Geneva more about his tactics. And, unrealized by that missionary in her final moments, she had ministered, through teaching and example, to her very last. Her life ended with a spiritual victory.

Geneva also had been privileged to be with her mother when she passed away. As well as allowing her to comfort her mother at this time, it also reconfirmed for Geneva the tenacity of mankind's spiritual enemy.

"I think it was the same evening she died," Geneva says. "My brother and I were with her. I was sitting by the bed. I sang songs to her and quoted scripture, but all of a sudden she opened her eyes, she looked at me and said, 'They are trying to deceive me!' And that was all she said. I said, 'Mother, is the devil trying to deceive you? ... Then I talked to her. I said, 'He has no power over you,' and I claimed a real prayer of victory over her. I told him to get out of that place. It shows how tremendously intent the devil is, even if he can't get the soul in that last hour, he will try to put doubts in their heads."

"He is merciless," Gordon says.

Which is why it could be such a blessing to have Geneva present at that final hour for Pat. As before, Geneva comforted her with words that had spiritual power: John 16:33; John 14; Psalm 23; Isaiah 26:3 and 40:31.

After Pat's death, the family gathered from around the country for the funeral. At the service, Gordon shared a poem Pat had given him, an adaptation of "'twas The Night Before Christmas" that discussed the Second Coming of Christ.

Gordon and Geneva got to spend much time with the family as well: children, brothers, sisters. They became friends with them, shared many of Pat's thoughts in her final years of life, and saw a tenderness and love build between the family members. On the last day in Bill's mobile home, the family gathered in a circle and prayed. It was a breakthrough for them and something Pat had prayed for in life.

Those are just some of the ways Gordon and Geneva have spent their retirement years. But Africa is always in their minds and hearts. When asked why they were returning to Africa in 1996, Gordon's smile beamed.

"We really feel God would have us do it, but there is a selfish reason, too. People there are receiving the Lord all the time. At a church visit, 10 to 50 could respond. It generates excitement among Christians. It's fun to see the abundant fruit. Here, every once in a while, someone is turning to the Lord. Picture your own church. If your excitement quotient was generated by the number of people turning to Christ weekly, where would you be? But the excitement quotient out there is so well determined by the literally 10s, 50s, hundreds of people coming to the Lord."

"It goes far more than excitement," Geneva says. "There is a joy that comes with it."

Was he saying, that after decades of working in Africa, he was finding American churches too *boring* for him?

Gordon laughed and was quick to answer. "It is boring to the hilt. I can't preach the way I like to. I like to go up and down the aisles."

That got Geneva laughing as well. "He's like a lion that has to be turned out of his cage every once and a while," she says.

And everyone knows where lions would choose to be.

"Give me Africa," Gordon says.

Gordon and Geneva, 1997.

Just A Word from the Christensens

We hope you have enjoyed the story of our lives, *Fire in Their Bones*. It was a pleasure relating story arfter story to the writer of the book, Philip Randall.

If you have not yet embarked on the greatest adventure of your life, which is a personal relationship with the Lord Jesus Christ, permit us to let you in on a big open secret: Christ is waiting just now for you to turn to Him and be forever His friend.

Let us remind you of the facts of eternal life;

1. God loves you and offers a wonderful plan for your life. See John 3:16 and John 10:10.
2. Man is sinful and separated from God. Therefore, he cannot know and experience God's love and plan for his life. See Romans 6:23.
3. Jesus Christ is God's only provision for man's sin. Through Him you can know and experience God's love and plan for you life. John 14:6.
4. We must individually receive Jesus Christ as Savior and Lord. Then we can know and experience God's love and plan for our lives. See John 3:1–8. See also Ephesians 2:8, 9.

Phone number: 954-474-8905
email: gjcgmc@juno.com

www.ingramcontent.com/pod-product-compliance
Lightning Source LLC
Chambersburg PA
CBHW050434240426
43661CB00055B/2384